Plant Care

THE BEST OF
FINE GARDENING

Plant Care

The Taunton Press

Cover photo: Delilah Smittle

Back-cover photos: left, Rita Buchanan; top and
bottom center, Susan Kahn; right, Mark Kane

for fellow enthusiasts

First printing: June 1994
Printed in the United States of America

A FINE GARDENING Book

FINE GARDENING® is a trademark of The Taunton Press, Inc.,
registered in the U.S. Patent and Trademark Office.

The Taunton Press
63 South Main Street
Box 5506
Newtown, CT 06470-5506

Library of Congress Cataloging-in-Publication Data

Plant care.
        p.   cm. — (The Best of Fine gardening)
    Articles originally published in Fine gardening magazine.
    "A Fine gardening book"— T.p. verso.
    Includes index.
    ISBN 1-56158-086-4
    1. Gardening. 2. Ornamental trees. 3. Ornamental shrubs.
    4. Perennials. 5. Grapes. I. Fine gardening. II. Series.
SB453.P565   1994   94-1840
635.9 — dc20   CIP

Contents

Introduction

Here are the best of the articles on plant care presented by *Fine Gardening* magazine in its first five years of publication.

In this beautifully illustrated collection, expert home gardeners, horticulturists and landscape contractors provide answers to many of the common questions that people have about the fundamentals of horticulture, from propagating new plants to pruning and dividing mature ones. Ranging from the tried-and-true to the innovative, the approaches recommended by the authors are sure to improve your gardening skills.

You'll find the articles in this collection especially helpful and inspiring because they are the work of enthusiasts, gardeners who have given much thought to the hows and whys of good horticulture. Sharing their hard-won experience, the authors tell you how to succeed with your own plants.

The editors of *Fine Gardening* hope you'll experiment with the ideas in this collection of articles. No matter which you choose to try, your efforts will be rewarded.

"The Best of *Fine Gardening*" series collects articles from back issues of *Fine Gardening* magazine. A note on p. 96 gives the date of first publication for each article; product availability, suppliers' addresses and prices may have changed since then. This book is the fifth in the series.

Starting With Seeds

Grow your choice of flowers and vegetables

by Rita Buchanan

My gardening year begins right after Christmas when all the seed catalogs arrive in the mailbox. Within weeks, I've ordered and received my seeds; gathered pots, flats and soil mixes; and set up the fluorescent lights. By spring I have anywhere from half a dozen to two or three dozen apiece of a hundred or so different kinds of plants ready for the garden.

There are many good reasons for starting your own seeds indoors. Germination rates are higher in controlled indoor conditions, and the seedlings are more likely to survive when they don't have to battle the elements, birds and bugs. Starting seeds indoors can give you a head start on crops such as tomatoes and peppers, so you can harvest earlier. It may be the only way you can grow plants whose time to maturity exceeds your growing season. Perennials that are started early can get established in the garden before the onset of summer heat and drought; some that otherwise wouldn't flower in the first year may do so with an early start.

I start seeds indoors for all these reasons, but for me the biggest attraction is being able to grow interesting species and varieties of flowers and vegetables that I find only in catalogs, not at garden centers. Finally, starting seeds indoors is fun, and it gets me gardening months before the last frost.

The methods and equipment I use for growing from seed are simple and inexpensive. My first job in horticulture, when I was fresh out of college, was working for a bedding-plant nursery where we started seedlings by the thousands. I've adapted the techniques I learned there into a system that works well at home and requires neither a lot of time nor a great deal of space. I tend my seedlings on weekends and at night after work, in the corner of a spare room. I sow the seeds at close spacing in small pots, transplant tiny seedlings to standard plastic six-packs and grow the plants under fluorescent lights until they're ready to go outdoors. Success, I've found, depends as much on the care I give the plants as on the equipment I use.

Most important is providing plenty of light. I don't try to grow seedlings on windowsills. They have to be right up against the glass to get enough light, even in a south-facing window, and that close to the glass they get overheated in the daytime and chilled at night. Instead, I raise my seedlings on a light stand, where conditions are uniform and easily controlled.

My light stand (shown on p. 12) is a simple A-frame that I built from pine 1x2s and plywood, with three 2-bulb fluorescent shop-light fixtures hanging from adjustable chains. It accommodates six flats easily, with room for a few spare pots around the edges. The stand fastens together with bolts and wing nuts. It takes about half an hour to assemble or disassemble the stand at the beginning or end of the seed-starting season; the rest of the year, I store the components in the back of a closet. As soon as I've put up my lights, I'm ready to start.

Sowing seeds

Timing—First, I look for information about each variety I'm growing. How long does it take the seeds to germinate? How long until the seedlings are ready to set out in the cold frame or the garden? Should they go out before or after the last frost? Usually I find this information on the packets, in catalogs and reference books, or in my own records. If I can't locate it in those places, I divide the seeds into two or three batches and sow them at intervals to see what works best.

I want the seedlings to be ready for the garden when the garden is ready for them. Sometimes I'm surprised by plants that grow much faster or slower than expected, but normally I end up with transplants that are about 4 in. to 6 in. tall (or wide, or long, depending on their growth form) when I plant them in the garden.

Here in Connecticut, I raise most seedlings indoors between February and May. When I lived in the milder climates of Texas and Virginia, I started right after New Year's. For fall crops, I often start a smaller batch in July or August, following the same techniques. I start slow-growing plants such as impatiens, begonias and leeks about 12 to 16 weeks before I want to put them in the ground. Most annual vegetable and flower crops, such as tomatoes and snapdragons, need about six to ten weeks before they can be set out. The fastest growers, such as cucumbers and calendulas, are big enough for the garden in just four weeks.

Soil mix—Like many gardeners, I enjoy measuring and blending ingredients to make my own soil media, and think bagged potting soil is the horticultural equivalent of cake mix. But for raising transplants, I buy commercial seed-starting mixes such as Jiffy-Mix or Pro-Mix at the garden center. They work just as well as homemade mixes do, and I don't have to spend time making them up. The commercial mixtures are composed of finely ground sphagnum peat moss and vermiculite, combined according to a formula developed years ago at Cornell University. The mixes are sterile—free of weed seeds and disease organisms. They're lightweight, even when wet, so they don't stress thin-walled plastic trays and flats. Both the peat moss and the vermiculite particles absorb and hold moisture readily, but extra water drains quickly through the large pore spaces. The fine, granular texture of the mix makes it easy to spread a very thin layer over newly sown seeds, to tease apart the roots when you're separating a batch of seedlings, and to fill in around the roots when you're transplanting into cell-packs.

You can sow seeds in all kinds of containers, from recycled milk jugs and yogurt cups to wooden flats, soil blocks or Styrofoam plug trays—anything that's shallow and drains well. I use 2-in. to 4-in. plastic pots, about 2 in. deep. It's easiest to provide the right light, temperature and watering if each kind of seed is in a separate pot. Depending on the size of the seeds and seedlings, I can sow as many as 100 seeds in a pot—that's the most I ever want of any one kind of plant.

To start, I put some soil mix in a plastic dishpan, add hot water from the tap and

Buchanan starts gardening well before the last frost, sowing seeds of dozens of varieties of ornamental and edible plants. Here she lines up tiny tomato seeds in the packet crease and taps them off one by one into the pot. Identified with plastic markers, the sown pots await watering in the tray behind.

stir thoroughly, then let it sit 12 to 24 hours. (Dry sphagnum moss absorbs water slowly; hot water speeds the process.) When you use the soil, it should be moist but not so wet that you can mold it into lumps or squeeze out water. If it's too wet, add more dry soil. The mix should flow freely off a spoon, like sugar. In fact, I use a spoon to fill each pot with soil, then tap the pot against a table to settle and level the soil about ½ in. from the top of the pot. Tapping is enough—pressing down on the surface packs soil into an airless, soggy mass where seedlings are prone to rot.

Sowing and germination—Don't sow seeds when you're not in the mood to space them carefully. Putting too many seeds in a pot, or putting them too close together, makes it hard to separate the individual plants when you transplant them. Also, crowded seedlings grow tall and skinny with weak stems, and are vulnerable to diseases. Unless the packet or experience warns me otherwise, I assume that nearly all the seeds will germinate. I sow 10% to 25% more seeds than I want

plants so I can choose the strongest for the garden.

I position seeds on the soil surface at least four times as far apart as they are wide. This is painstaking work if the seeds are tiny. For them, I fold a sharp crease in the paper packet and line the seeds up single-file in the fold. Then I tap them off one at a time, or use a pencil to nudge each seed off the edge. For tiny dark-colored seeds, I sometimes spread a thin layer of white sand (sold as playbox sand) on the soil before sowing so I can see where the seeds land.

Seed germination is affected by light. Most tiny seeds, and even some medium-size seeds such as coleus and impatiens, germinate better if they're exposed to light. Only a few plants, including vinca and delphinium, demand total darkness. In most cases, even if there's too much or too little light, some of the seeds will germinate anyway, although germination may take longer. If a seed packet or catalog says that germination requires light, I leave the seeds uncovered; if darkness is

needed, I cover them with about ¼ in. of soil mix. If no light requirement is specified, I spread a shallow covering of soil—about a tablespoonful of mix for a 3-in. pot—over the surface, to help keep the seeds moist. Then, so I won't lose track, I write the plant name and the date with indelible ink on a plastic plant label and insert it along the edge of the pot.

Next I settle the seeds into place by sprinkling the surface of the pot with water from a hand-held rubber watering bulb. This has to be a very gentle spray—using a hose or a sprinkling can would wash a hole in the surface, pack down the soil and flood the seeds out of position. I put the pots close together in a standard nursery flat and set it on the light stand. (Sold at most garden centers, these flats are called "1020" flats, although they actually measure 11 in. by 22 in. by 2 in. deep.) Indoors, I use flats without drain holes so water won't spill out the bottom and onto the floor.

It's important that seeds stay evenly moist until they germinate. A good way to achieve this is to put the pots in a mini-greenhouse. I use a clear-plastic dome made to cover a standard nursery flat, but placing the pots inside a clear-plastic shoebox or sweater box would also work. I've had no luck putting individual pots inside plastic sandwich bags; every time I've tried it, I've ended up with weak seedlings and scumlike growths of algae and mold on the surface of the soil. The miniature greenhouse will keep the seeds moist for several weeks without additional watering, which is long enough for most seeds to germinate.

Like light or darkness, some seeds prefer warm or cool conditions for germination, but again, there's usually a range of acceptable temperature. Most vegetable and flower seeds germinate readily if the soil temperature is between 70° and 80°F. Since the temperature in my workroom drops into the low sixties at night, I put the domed flat on a heating pad or a heat cable to warm the soil from underneath. It doesn't matter if the air is cool, as long as the soil stays warm. Garden centers and seed catalogs offer a variety of electric soil-heating cables and mats. Look for a heating device with a built-in thermostat preset at about 74°F.

Under these conditions, many vegetable and flower seeds germinate in two to 30 days. I check each pot daily and look for emerging shoots. Seedlings are most vulnerable to neglect immediately after germination, while they're still tiny. As soon as shoots appear, I take the pot off the heat and out of the mini-greenhouse, so the plants aren't softened by high temperature and humidity. If some seeds haven't germinated after five to six weeks, and I suspect that I've made a mistake with water, light or temperature, I empty out the pot and try again. Sometimes, however, I've been surprised by seedlings on the compost pile—I just hadn't given them enough time.

Raising seedlings

Environment—Like germination, good growth depends on light and temperature. Three aspects of light are important: quality, intensity and duration. The quality, or wavelengths, of light provided by ordinary fluorescent bulbs are satisfactory for growing seedlings. You don't need to buy the costlier "grow lights" or full-spectrum bulbs.

The intensity, or brightness, of the light is greatest close to the source. While the seedlings are less than 1 in. tall, I'm careful to keep them positioned within 2 in. of the tubes. As they grow taller, I keep adjusting the pots and the lights, trying to keep the light bulbs 2 in. to 6 in. above the top of the leaves. Not getting enough light is what makes seedlings "leggy." Putting them close to the bulbs is important. Also, I give them 18 hours of light a day. I plug the lights into a 24-hour timer (avail-

able at hardware stores), and set it to switch on at 6:00 a.m. and off at midnight.

Fluorescent lights don't give off much heat, so the temperature on the light stand usually is about the same as the room temperature. I set a minimum/maximum recording thermometer next to the plants and check each day's high and low. If the air temperature is 50° to 65°F at night and 60° to 75°F in the daytime, most seedlings do fine.

Water and fertilizer—Careful watering is a necessity for seedlings, especially at the early stages, as I've learned and relearned the hard way. There's no safe way to water a whole flat full of assorted seedlings at once. Some pots will need watering every few days, others less than once a week. It all depends on the kind of plant, how many there are in the pot and how big they are. By far the best way to water is one pot at a time. If a pot feels lightweight and the soil color is light, I know it's time to water.

I fill a shallow bowl with tepid water and lower the pot in the bowl to absorb water from the bottom up. A few seconds' dip will saturate the soil, and that's enough. As soon as I see a color change on the surface of the soil, I pull up the pot and let the excess water drain away before replacing the pot in the flat. Well-timed bottom watering is important for the roots. They grow deeper and stronger if the soil begins to dry out on top between waterings but still has moisture near the bottom.

Also, keeping the surface of the soil dry helps protect the stems from "damping-off." This is a fungal disease that destroys the stem tissue right at the soil line, so the seedlings flop over and die. Damping-off can level a pot of seedlings in just a few hours. The spores that cause damping-off are ubiquitous, so sterilizing pots and soil is a temporary measure, and fungicides offer only limited protection. Sowing the seeds far enough apart that air can circulate between the young plants is helpful, but the best way I've found to prevent damping-off is to always water pots of seedlings from the bottom up.

Some seed-starting mixes contain nutrients; some don't. Either way, I start fertilizing as soon as the seedlings have two or more true leaves, and I continue until I set them out into the garden. Once a week, I add ¼ tsp. of soluble fertilizer, such as Peters 20-20-20 or 15-30-15, per gallon of irrigation water. Some people use manure tea, fish emulsion or seaweed extract. I don't think the source of nutrients matters, but feeding frequently with one product or another helps promote steady, vigorous growth.

Transplanting—I transplant seedlings after they've grown two or more true leaves (cotyledons don't count), which can be two to six weeks after germina-

tion. Transplanting is close and careful work—I sit at a well-lit table. In the process of giving each little plant its own pot, I notice details I'd never see from farther away. Those first true leaves are remarkably characteristic of the species. Even when the plants are less than an inch tall, you can recognize the pungent fragrance of marigolds, the crisp texture of wax begonias, the feathery shape of dill, and the bright red or gold stems of celosia.

Freeing a seedling from its neighbors in a pot can be daunting if you haven't done it before. The little plants look so fragile. One precaution is to always grasp a plant by a leaf, not the stem. The plant can survive loss or injury of a leaf, but it's fatal to snap the stem. The real problem in separating seedlings is disentangling the roots. Here's where I appreciate the fine texture of seed-starting soil mixes, as it allows the seedlings to come apart with minimum root breakage.

If I have a pot full of dozens of delicate tiny seedlings, such as begonias or petunias, I start at one edge and lift them out one at a time, using a pencil to prod and free the roots. If the seedlings are an inch or more tall, their roots will be too long for this procedure. Instead, I turn over the whole pot, carefully pull out the soil ball, then untangle each plant from its neighbors.

It's very tempting to pot up every single seedling that germinates, but it's better not to, unless you have a lot of space. A 4-in. pot's worth of seedlings can expand into a few square feet of six-packs after transplanting, and several square yards or more of garden space by mid-summer. I often spread a batch of seedlings on a sheet of paper as I separate them, count how many there are, and think about how many I have room for in the garden. Then I choose the sturdiest, most uniform plants, and regretfully discard the others.

You can transplant seedlings into all sorts of containers—it's a matter of personal choice. I use preformed plastic six-packs. Six is a convenient number of plants to handle, and often all I want of something. The packs are modular and use space efficiently, and you can mix or match packs of different cell sizes in the same flat. Six-packs are inexpensive or come free from plant-buying friends, easy to clean and sterilize for reuse (I wash them in hot soapy water with a jigger of bleach), and compact to store from year to year. Of all the systems I've tried, I think transplants come out of these containers with the least root disturbance.

The size of the plants and their rate of growth determines what size pot to put them into. I use six-packs with three different cell sizes—1¼ in. square, 1¼ in. by 2½ in., and 2½ in. square (all are 2 in. deep)—for dainty, average and robust

It's possible to start dozens of seedlings in a 2-in. or 3-in. pot (top left). Soon after they've formed their first true leaves, they're ready for transplanting into individual pots. Seedlings at this stage of growth have different-size root systems, depending on the species of plant and the soil moisture. Some plants, like this sweet basil (top right), make roots that far exceed their top growth, especially if the soil is allowed to dry out between waterings. (Other plants may have smaller roots, particularly if grown in damp soil.)

As she separates a potful of seedlings, Buchanan holds each plant by a leaf and uses a pencil to untangle the roots. To transplant plants with small root systems, like this dianthus (right), she pokes a hole in the soil mix, inserts the plant and draws the soil around it. When transplanting seedlings with large root systems, like this pansy (above), she suspends the plant in the center of an empty cell and spoons soil mix in around it.

Photos: top right, Robert Marsala; others, Staff

plants, respectively. When in doubt, I choose a smaller-size pot, because it's better for roots to quickly fill the volume of soil in a cell than to be surrounded with excess soil that stays wet.

There are two methods of transplanting. If the root system is large, or the roots are thick and brittle, hold the plant with one hand, suspending the roots in the center of an empty pot, and spoon in pre-moistened seed-starting soil with your other hand. Fill the pot level with the rim, then gently tamp around the edge. If the root system is small, or the roots are thin and fibrous, fill the pot first with loose soil, make a hole in the middle with a pencil or your finger, drop the roots into the hole, then draw the soil back in and tamp it into place.

I usually set a seedling deeper than it was in the germination pot, placing the cotyledons just above the soil surface. (Seedlings of sweet peas, lilies, grasses and other plants whose cotyledons stay below the soil surface should be replanted at the same depth as they were before.) Some plants will form roots along the section of the stem that's buried when you transplant deeper; others won't. Either way, setting the seedlings deeper

helps hold them in an upright position, so they don't flop over.

Maintenance—The flats of six-packs go on the light stand. Every week or two, I move six-packs from one flat to another, to group like-size seedlings together. This way, it's easier for me to keep the leaves uniformly close to the lights. Big plants dry out faster than small plants do; segregating them by size also reduces the incidence of under- or overwatering. Given these needs, it's fun to combine plants of different colors and textures to see how they look together.

I prefer to water the six-packs like I water pots of seedlings: from the bottom. If all the packs in a flat are similarly dry, I pour water into the flat and let them soak it up. I make sure to pour excess water out of the flat afterward, so the roots don't stay too wet. If only a few packs look dry, I dip them into a separate dish of water and replace them. As seedlings grow bigger, they're more tolerant of overhead watering, but still vulnerable to overwatering.

If I need to go away for a few days during the spring and I can arrange it, I plan to go right after sowing a batch of seeds, or right after transplanting seedlings into six-packs, when they can go

without watering for as long as a week. Another way to provide water while you're away is with a layer of capillary matting in the bottom of the flats. It's a puffy, synthetic-fiber fabric that absorbs moisture and releases it gradually to the drying soil. (Most mail-order seed companies sell capillary mats.) In my experience, matting will hold enough water to last more than a week.

Sometimes I underestimate how fast or how big a batch of seedlings will grow, and have to pot them up again before it's time for them to go in the garden. I repot plants if they're tippy (more than three times as tall as the pots), if they dry out and need watering more than once daily, or if the leaves and stems in a six-pack are getting tangled together. If the seedlings get way too big, and I don't have room for them, I may save just a few and have to discard the rest.

Sometimes seedlings do poorly. Pests can cause problems, but I've been able to kill aphids and spider mites by spraying them with a solution of insecticidal soap. Often it's hard to identify the cause of sickly plants. A soil pH that's too high or too low, nutrient excess or deficiency, temperature extremes, and under- or

Lightweight light stand

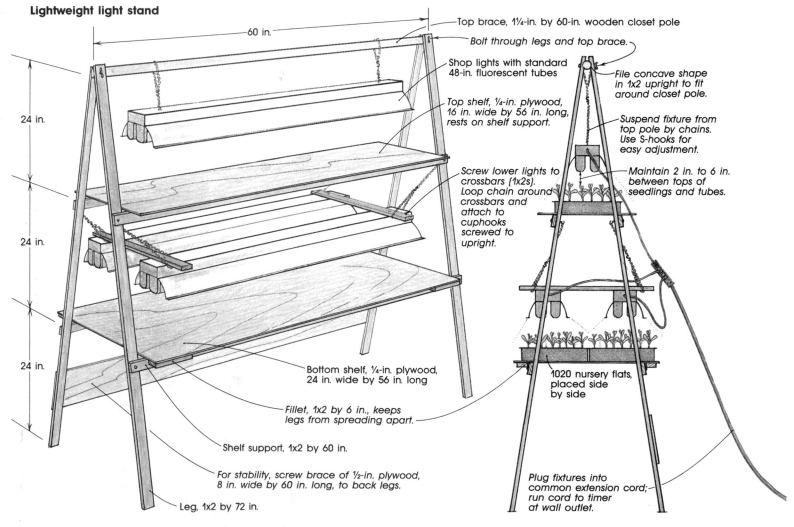

60 in.

24 in.

24 in.

24 in.

Top brace, 1¼-in. by 60-in. wooden closet pole

Bolt through legs and top brace.

Shop lights with standard 48-in. fluorescent tubes

Top shelf, ¼-in. plywood, 16 in. wide by 56 in. long, rests on shelf support.

Screw lower lights to crossbars (1x2s). Loop chain around crossbars and attach to cuphooks screwed to upright.

File concave shape in 1x2 upright to fit around closet pole.

Suspend fixture from top pole by chains. Use S-hooks for easy adjustment.

Maintain 2 in. to 6 in. between tops of seedlings and tubes.

Bottom shelf, ¼-in. plywood, 24 in. wide by 56 in. long

1020 nursery flats, placed side by side

Fillet, 1x2 by 6 in., keeps legs from spreading apart.

Shelf support, 1x2 by 60 in.

For stability, screw brace of ½-in. plywood, 8 in. wide by 60 in. long, to back legs.

Leg, 1x2 by 72 in.

Plug fixtures into common extension cord; run cord to timer at wall outlet.

Illustration: Staff

Weeks or months of indoor effort are rewarded when the seedlings are transplanted into the garden (right and below).

overwatering are all manifested in a few redundant symptoms such as discolored leaves and weak growth. I try to learn what went wrong, for the sake of knowledge, but I don't nurse sick seedlings. There's not much invested and not much lost if I dump them out and start again.

Planting out

When my light stand gets full, I "graduate" the biggest, oldest, most cold-tolerant plants out to a cold frame so I can start new batches of seedlings under the lights. This doubles my growing area, and provides a transition between indoors and outdoors. If you don't have a cold frame, keep your seedlings under the lights until you can put them outdoors. Remember that bright light is essential for growing sturdy seedlings—don't set them around as if they were houseplants.

Plants grown in the protected environment of a house or a cold frame have soft leaves and stems. Before transplanting them into the garden, it's best to harden them off, gradually exposing them to hotter and colder temperatures, bright sun, drying winds, and overhead watering. At first, set them out for only an hour or so in the morning or afternoon, then leave them out all day, and finally leave them out day and night. This is a critical time for seedling survival, especially because they dry out very quickly and may need watering more than once a day. Often I have to water both before and after work. I'll spend a week hardening the seedlings off, then put them in the garden, weather permitting.

Depending on my schedule and the weather forecast, I try to set plants into the garden just before a spell of cloudy weather. It's easiest to transplant seedlings out of six-packs if the soil in the cells is just starting to dry out, so the root ball comes out intact. If the soil is quite wet, the root ball is more liable to break apart. Sometimes I have to reach underneath and push up if the roots are sticking to the edges of the cell, but usually I can just lift a plant out by its stem. Rarely does a plant break when I'm trying to get it out of the six-pack.

I use a narrow trowel to dig a hole the size of the root ball, and set the plant in place. Then I pull garden soil over the top of the potting soil and around the stem, and water well to settle the soil around the roots. I finish by mixing a sprinkling can of fertilizer solution and applying some to the leaves of each plant. Unless cutworms, late frost or other hazards intervene, the plants grow and thrive. □

Rita Buchanan is an associate editor at Fine Gardening.

Photos: Steve Buchanan

Breaking Dormancy

How to find what it takes to get a seed to grow

by James A. and Cheryl G. Young

Compared to starting common garden annuals such as tomatoes and zinnias, it's frequently a challenge to raise native plants from seeds. Garden-variety seeds usually germinate promptly if supplied with moisture and warmth. By contrast, the seeds of many native plants may lie dormant for years until particular environmental conditions trigger germination. The challenge for would-be growers is to determine just what these conditions are. Only occasionally can you find the answer in reference books. Often you have to figure it out on your own.

We've spent the last 25 years researching native plants and have identified the conditions that break dormancy in hundreds of different species. Unraveling dormancy problems is like detective work; we use a systematic approach to test one clue after another. The many types of dormancy respond to many different conditions. This article describes the treatments that are most commonly effective.

Research like this doesn't require a fancy lab—you can use the same approach at home to start seeds you collect from wildflowers, shrubs and trees. If you know something about a plant from reading or from previous experience, you may anticipate which treatments will be most effective. If you're starting with a new kind of plant, divide the supply of seeds into small lots to test in different ways.

When we're testing seeds to identify what treatment(s) will overcome their dormancy, we have to be able to observe the results. So rather than sowing them in a soil mix, we place the seeds on a sheet of damp blotter paper in clear-plastic petri dishes. You can substitute paper coffee filters for the blotter paper, but don't use roll-type paper towels, as they may have germicide. For containers, use plastic freezer boxes or the clear-plastic serving dishes from delicatessens. It's easiest if you invert the container, spread the seeds on the lid and use the bottom as a greenhouselike dome.

As soon as a batch of seeds begins to sprout, we gently transfer them to a pot, flat or seedbed of prepared soil where the seedlings can continue to grow. Seedlings aren't shocked by transplanting if you do it when the radicle—the tiny embryonic root—has just barely emerged. Breaking dormancy is just the first step in raising plants from seeds, but it's often the most frustrating and puzzling one. Once you get the seeds started, chances are you can grow the plants to maturity.

Seeds and fruits of native plants have a visible diversity of size and color (facing page; seeds are shown about twice life size), and an invisible diversity of dormancy mechanisms. Collecting seeds is easy. The challenge is breaking dormancy and getting them to germinate.

In order to see the effects of different treatments on overcoming dormancy, try sowing seeds on a layer of absorbent paper. Spread the paper in a plastic food container that can be closed to retain moisture. As soon as the seeds begin to sprout, gently transfer them to a pot or flat of soil mix.

ARE THE SEEDS VIABLE?

The term "viable" means that a seed is alive and capable of germinating once dormancy is broken. If a seed isn't viable, it's dead. We check the seeds' appearance as the first clue to their viability: if they're discolored, cracked or shrunken, or show insect damage, they may not be viable.

Of course, the ultimate proof of viability is germination itself, but it's possible to assess the viability of still-dormant seeds by observing their susceptibility to infection by fungi and bacteria. Place a few seeds on moist blotter paper in a closed container and incubate them at room temperature (approximately 60° to

75°F). After a week's time, microorganisms will have begun to colonize the blotter paper, but clear areas should remain around viable seeds, which seem to have a chemical defense against infection. Dead seeds will be covered with a growth of microorganisms after the same incubation period.

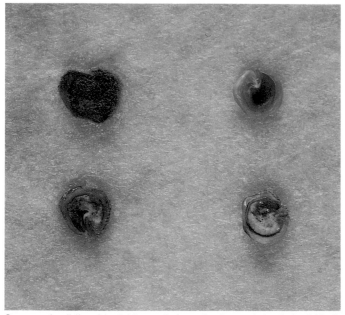

One way to distinguish viable seeds from dead ones is by their ability to resist infection. Within a week after these prickly-pear seeds were spread on damp paper, three dead seeds have become covered with fungi and bacteria. The live seed (top right) has resisted contamination.

DO THE SEEDS NEED MORE TIME?

Many seeds are dormant when freshly harvested, but the dormancy is lost over time (a period of days to months, depending on the species). After-ripening is a term for this gradual loss of dormancy. The need to after-ripen implies that the embryo is not yet mature when the seed is harvested.

To test whether the seeds simply need more time, sow small test batches one, two and three months after harvest. If germination increases with each subsequent test, you can be sure that the seeds are after-ripening. This type of dormancy is very common among grass species. No special treatments are needed, just patience. If you wait, nature will solve the problem.

CAN THE SEEDS TAKE UP WATER?

Seeds can't germinate until the embryo and stored food take up or imbibe water. This isn't a problem for most soft seeds, but hard seeds may have impermeable seed coats that impede the uptake of water. To test for dormancy caused by impermeable seed coats, put the seeds on moist blotter paper for a few days, then try to slice them with a single-edge razor blade or a very sharp knife. A plump and relatively easy-to-cut seed is fully imbibed and ready for planting or further testing.

If the seed coat and its contents are still hard, the seeds need some form of scarification, a treatment that consists of scarring or breaking the hard seed coat. If the seeds you're working with are large enough to hold, the simplest method of scarification is to chip through each seed coat with a sharp blade, or to nick it with a fine-tooth file. In most cases it's best to nick the side away

Some seeds have hard, impermeable seed coats that prevent water up-take. Chipping away a bit of the seed coat will allow these seeds of Texas mountain laurel to imbibe water and germinate.

from the embryo. If you can't tell from the outside where the embryo is located, dissect one or two seeds to find out. Or, nick several seeds in different places and hope for the best.

Commercial processors who handle large quantities of seeds often use mechanical scarifiers, which rub the seeds against an abrasive surface. Sandpaper-covered blocks of wood do the same job for small lots of seeds. The risk of mechanical scarification is that it's hard to control—it can result in damage to the embryo and do more harm than good. Hot-water treatment is a safer method of scarification. Bring a quart of water to a boil, remove the pot from the heat and immediately drop in up to a

Another way to deal with impermeable seed coats is to shock the seeds with hot water. Drop the seeds, like these of honey locust, into scalding water, and let them cool in the water for 24 hours before planting them.

handful of seeds. Then allow the seeds to soak overnight in the cooling water.

Seeds scarified by pricking, sanding or the hot-water treatment should be thoroughly imbibed within a day or two. Plant them immediately without letting them dry out. Scarification often leads to germination, but success isn't guaranteed. Sometimes a seed will imbibe water, but the embryo may still lie dormant. If the scarified seeds don't germinate, they may need further treatment.

DOES COOL-MOIST STRATIFICATION HELP?

In nature, many seeds pass the winter atop nonfrozen soil under continuous snow cover. They remain dormant during this period of cool-moist conditions, then germinate in the spring. Prechilling, or stratification, duplicates the conditions these seeds need to overcome dormancy. (The term "stratification" comes from the forestry practice of layering tree seeds among damp peat—the alternating layers have the appearance of geologic strata—before chilling them in a refrigerator.) Note that moisture is a crucial part of the procedure. Storing dry seeds at cold temperatures is not effective.

An easy way to stratify small batches of seeds is to place them in a plastic bag with some damp peat moss, perlite or vermiculite. There should be a little free water visible at the bottom of the bag. Label the bag with the plant species and date, and put it in the refrigerator, where the temperature range is normally between 32° and 40°F.

Many seeds need prolonged exposure to cool and moist conditions to overcome dormancy. A treatment called stratification meets this requirement. Place the seeds in a bag of damp peat moss, and store it in the refrigerator.

How long should seeds be stratified? Requirements for specific seeds range from a few days to several months, but a month to six weeks is most common. If you have no idea how long the seeds will need, place subsamples in individual plastic bags and periodically remove them for planting. Start with two-week intervals; if you go past six weeks, increase the time between recoveries to a month. Examine the seeds when you remove them from stratification. If the radicles are beginning to emerge from the seed coats, it's time to plant the entire seed lot. Further stratification will eventually reduce germination. Plant stratified seeds promptly, without letting them dry out, in a

seedbed conducive to continued growth.

An old trick used by nurserymen in northern environments is to soak conifer seeds overnight in water and then bury them in snow for four to six weeks before planting. It works very well in areas with prolonged snow cover. Another approach is to plant the seeds in flats of damp sand, cover them with vermiculite or another moisture-holding mulch, and overwinter the flats outside on the north side of a building. This technique may not lead to full germination, but it will often produce a few seedlings.

Sometimes you can bypass the requirement for cool-moist stratification by simply cutting open the seeds and dissecting out the embryos. If you need just a few plants, this is a shortcut alternative to cool-moist stratification. Soak the seeds overnight to soften the coats, and try your luck with a dissecting needle. Place the dissected embryos in a clean, closed dish on moist blotter paper. As long as the embryos aren't damaged severely, seedlings can develop even from rather ragged-looking dissected specimens.

IS LIGHT REQUIRED?

Most kinds of seeds germinate best in the dark, but a few (particularly tiny seeds) require light for germination. If you've gotten this far and the seeds still fail to germinate, it's time to try putting them under light.

Different wavelengths of light have different effects. Shorter wavelengths of red light stimulate germination; the longer wavelengths of far-red light inhibit germination. To be exact in working with light and seed germination, we use safelights, filters, light-proof boxes and a host of other equipment in the lab. At home, it's enough to remember that light from cool fluorescent tubes or bulbs enhances germination, while light from warm incandescent bulbs inhibits germination. Try placing a few seeds on moist paper in a container such as a pie tin and covering the tin with plastic wrap. This will let in light while protecting the seeds from moisture loss. Put the container within several inches of a fluorescent light fixture, and supply light for about eight hours a day.

WHAT ABOUT THE TEMPERATURE?

Certain seeds germinate better when day and night temperatures differ by a range of 35° to 40°F. You can meet their needs by putting the seed-starting container in the coldest portion of the refrigerator at night, then placing it in a warm room during the daytime, until the seeds germinate. Seeds that have this type of dormancy are usually very reluctant to germinate before treatment, but have high germination afterward. Desert salt grass is one plant that responds dramatically to this temperature-shift treatment.

WILL CHEMICALS HELP?

All the previous tests—breaking seed coats, chilling, adding light, and varying the temperature—are physical methods of enhancing germination. Wouldn't it be easier if there were some magic chemical that could be sprinkled on the seeds to instantly overcome dormancy? Well, this doesn't happen very often, but there are a few chemicals that in proper concentration can remarkably enhance germination.

The nitrate ion is probably the most influential, and it's the easiest for a home gardener to experiment with. The form most

Steps in overcoming dormancy

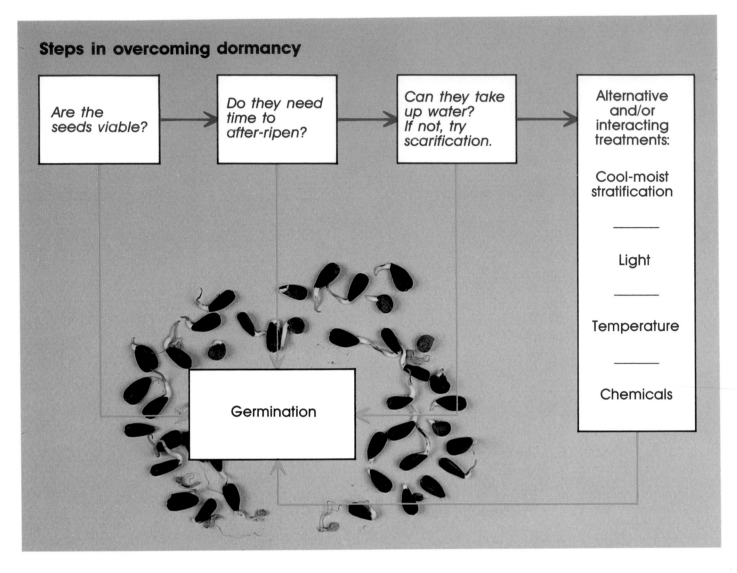

| Are the seeds viable? | → | Do they need time to after-ripen? | → | Can they take up water? If not, try scarification. | → | Alternative and/or interacting treatments:

Cool-moist stratification

———

Light

———

Temperature

———

Chemicals |

Germination

commonly used is potassium nitrate. The maximum recommended concentration is a 0.2% solution (roughly one level teaspoon per gallon), as too much nitrate is toxic to germination and plant growth. Apply the solution to the blotting paper under the seeds or to the sowing mix. Alyssum, cleome, California poppy and cosmos are plants whose seeds respond to nitrate enrichment.

Gibberellic acid is a plant hormone that can greatly enhance germination of certain seeds. (It's available from Mellinger's, Inc., 2310 W. South Range Rd., North Lima, OH 44452; cost is $2.79 for 4 oz.) The solution, however, must be very dilute—1 to 2 parts per million—and is difficult to mix without a laboratory balance. A too-high concentration of gibberellic acid causes seedlings to be very elongated and weak. Furthermore, since gibberellic acid breaks down very quickly at room temperatures, the solution must be fresh to be effective. Combining equal parts of potassium nitrate and gibberellic acid solutions solves the weak-seedling problem, and in most cases it's synergistic for enhancing germination.

COMBINE TREATMENTS.

Dormant seeds may often benefit from more than one treatment. For example, cool-moist stratification can be made more effective and/or of shorter duration if the stratification substrate is enriched with potassium nitrate, gibberellic acid or a mixture of both. In some cases one or both of these chemicals can be

substituted for cool-moist stratification requirements or even for light requirements.

Not only can individual seeds have multiple types of dormancy, but a given plant species can produce different types of seeds—larger or smaller, light- or dark-colored—that have different types of dormancy. These different kinds of seeds respond to different treatments, but all produce the same plants. When gardeners write us for advice on germinating dormant seeds, they frequently say that they were very careful when they cleaned their seeds; they threw all the small or lighter-colored seeds away and kept only the large dark ones. More often than not, they may have thrown away the seed form that germinates readily, and kept the highly dormant seeds. Don't discard any forms of a mixed lot of seeds until you've tested them all for germination.

Inducing a dormant seed to germinate can be challenging, and it's easy to get frustrated on particularly difficult species. When we get to an impasse, we go back and study the conditions where the plant grows in nature, looking for a new clue as to what its seeds might respond to or require. Then we collect more seeds and try again. The rewards, both in knowledge and in new plants for the garden, are well worth pursuing. □

James A. and Cheryl G. Young study native plants in Reno, Nevada. They're the authors of Collecting, Processing, and Germinating the Seeds of Wildland Plants *(Timber Press, Portland, Oregon; 1986).*

Storing Seeds

Use desiccants to keep them dry

by Bruce Bugbee

Despite their inert appearance, seeds are actually living organisms. How long they stay alive, able to germinate and grow into new plants, depends on the conditions—especially temperature and moisture levels—they are exposed to. Seeds deteriorate quickly at normal room temperatures and humidity. In a paper packet on the shelf, onion seeds lose their viability in a year, corn and pepper seeds in two years, beans and peas in three years. Kept cool and dry, however, seeds will germinate as well after decades of storage as they do when they are fresh.

Proper storage conditions maintain a

high germination percentage, and also maintain seed vigor (that is, a seed's ability to germinate and grow rapidly even under stress). Low-vigor seeds are alive, but they produce good plants only when conditions are favorable. For example, they may germinate in a warm greenhouse but not in cold soil in the garden. Seed vigor is difficult to measure, but in storage it declines more rapidly than does germination percentage.

Whether you're saving leftover packets from one year to the next or preserving germplasm for future generations, the methods are the same. My colleague Gus

Seeds can be stored successfully for decades in cool, dry conditions. Author Bugbee seals his seeds inside waterproof glass or plastic containers (above), enclosing a small packet of a desiccant such as silica gel or calcium alumino-silicate clay to keep moisture levels below 5%.

Koerner and I have developed a system for storing seeds that's inexpensive, practical and very effective. We use a desiccant, or drying compound, to reduce the moisture content of the seeds, and store them in waterproof containers. Then we set the containers in a cool place, often in a refrigerator or a freezer.

The effects of moisture and temperature

I got interested in seeds as a student. One of my former teachers, Dr. Jim Harrington at the University of California in Davis, did research on seed physiology and seed storage. He found that seed storage life approximately doubles with each 1% decrease in seed moisture, and doubles again for every 9°F decrease in temperature. This rule of thumb applies to seeds containing between 5% and 14% moisture, at temperatures between 32° and

A COMPARISON OF DESICCANT EFFICIENCY

Desiccant	Efficiency	Approximate cost per lb.	Cost per lb. of water absorbed
Powdered milk	5%	$1.80	$36.00
Drierite (calcium sulfate)	10%	2.25	22.50
Activated alumina	12%	12.00	98.00
Silica gel alone	33%	4.00	12.00
Silica gel with cobalt chloride	33%	8.00	24.00
Calcium alumino-silicate clay	35%	1.80	5.00
Magnesium perchlorate	40%	22.00	55.00

122°F. (Temperatures below freezing improve storage life, but they don't necessarily double the life for each 9°F decrease. Reducing the moisture level below about 3% is not recommended.)

Moisture and temperature have independent effects, and the effects are additive. For example, sweet-corn seeds kept in a paper envelope in a room with 60% relative humidity contain about 10% moisture. If the temperature of the room is 68°F, the vigor of the corn seeds will decrease noticeably after two years. But if the seeds are dried to a moisture content of 5% and are kept in a moisture-proof container, the storage life will increase by 32 times over that of the seeds in the envelope. If the moisture-proof jar is put in a freezer at 32°F, the storage life will increase an additional 16 times. The total increase in storage life will be 32 plus 16, or 48 times. Thus, Harrington's equation predicts that the drier, colder corn seeds will retain their vigor and viability for 96 years, which is 48 times as long as the seeds on the shelf. This equation has been validated by considerable seed-storage data.

We put this knowledge into practice in designing our seed-storage system. The ideal storage environment is cold and dry. Temperature is easy to measure and control. Putting seeds in the freezer is better than putting them in the refrigerator, and the refrigerator is better than on the shelf. Providing cold temperatures, however, can quickly get expensive. It is much cheaper to reduce seed moisture.

Unlike temperature, seed moisture is difficult to measure, but it can be predicted because it reaches an equilibrium with the relative humidity of the air, and that is easy to measure. Stored in a room with 60% average relative humidity, seeds have a moisture content of 7% to 12%. This is far too high for good storage. Relative humidities in the western United States are lower than those in the East, but still too high for good seed storage. For best storage, seeds should be kept in an environment with a relative humidity of less than 10%, and have a moisture content of less than 5%.

SOURCES

For small quantities of silica gel or "Humisorb" calcium alumino-silicate clay:
Bill Beckman, Delta Industries, 1000 Industrial Dr., Unit 1-C, Bensonville, IL 60106. 312-595-3205. Price list free.

For small quantities of "Desi Pak" calcium alumino-silicate clay:
Ralph Muth, Muth Associates, 53 Progress Ave., Springfield, MA 01104. 413-734-2107. One container of 25 bags costs $20.00 plus $4.00 shipping.

For silica gel with the blue/pink color indicator:
John Quinn, P.O. Box 2924, Petaluma, CA 94953. 707-778-0567. An 8-oz. bag costs $3.25 postpaid; 16 oz. costs $5.25 postpaid.

For humidity-indicator paper treated with cobalt chloride, which you can use in combination with any desiccant:
Robert Crossno, The Humidial Corporation, P.O. Box 464, Colton, CA 92324. 714-825-1793. Catalog free; inquire about retail distributors in your area.

Desiccants

We use desiccants to control seed moisture levels—to draw excess moisture out of seeds, and to keep seeds dry inside a sealed container. Desiccant compounds can be saturated with moisture, and then be dried out and reused, thousands of times, apparently forever.

Many types of desiccants are available, differing in efficiency and cost. We've made some measurements and calculations to compare different kinds. We measure efficiency as a percent, equal to the weight of water absorbed per weight of desiccant. This figure, as well as the approximate cost for enough of each desiccant to absorb 1 lb. of water, is given in the table above.

Of the six desiccants we've tested, silica gel and calcium alumino-silicate clay are the most useful for seed savers. I used to recommend using powdered milk as a desiccant, but I don't anymore. It's relatively inefficient and expensive. Also, it's liable to go rancid and can't be recycled indefinitely as other desiccants can. Silica gel is a very good desiccant, and it's rela-

tively efficient and economical. You can order it by mail (see Sources). The calcium alumino-silicate clay is a special kind of montmorillonite clay that is mined in Oklahoma and New Mexico and marketed under trade names such as "Desi Pak" and "Humisorb." At the low humidities that occur in sealed storage, this clay has almost twice the water-holding capacity of silica gel.

You can't tell by looking or feeling if a desiccant is wet or dry, unless it's been treated with an indicator. Silica gel is often treated with cobalt chloride, a humidity indicator that changes from a deep blue when it's dry (below about 5% moisture) to light pink when it's saturated (above about 40% moisture), with shades of lavender in between. Indicator-treated silica gel costs more, because cobalt chloride is quite expensive, but it's definitely worth the price. The calcium alumino-silicate clay desiccant cannot be treated, but some manufacturers put a piece of paper that contains cobalt chloride in with the desiccant. You can buy treated humidity-indicator paper to use with any desiccant. Or, you can use a little bit of treated silica gel in combination with the untreated clay, to get the benefits of the indicator.

Storage containers

Seeds must be stored in waterproof or water-resistant containers. Paper envelopes or cloth bags cannot be used, because water vapor passes readily through them. Air inside the storage container must be very dry. Some companies, such as Park Seed, use waterproof foil packets, but once you've broken the seal, moisture gradually enters those packets, too.

It's a good idea to put all your seed packets inside a larger, waterproof container. We've tested several kinds. Some moisture penetrates into any container, sooner or later, by diffusing through the walls or leaking through the seal. To determine how fast moisture is leaking in, put a quarter of a teaspoon of desiccant in the container along with some cobalt chloride moisture indicator. If the cobalt chloride is still deep blue after a week, the container is adequately sealed.

Plastics are slightly permeable to water vapor, but penetration through heavy plastic is very slow. Thick polyethylene containers with tight-fitting, snap-on lids are suitable, and even zip-lock storage bags are adequate. Glass jars with rubber-gasketed metal lids are excellent if the lids are screwed on tight. Old coffee cans make good containers, but they leak at the seal between the plastic and the metal. We have made coffee cans moisture-resistant by wrapping the seal with two layers of black electrical tape. We tested an ice chest and found its built-in seal was inadequate, but putting closed-cell (not open-cell, which leaks) foam weatherstripping around the lid made it very moisture-resistant.

Drying fresh seeds

If you're saving seeds from your own plants, you'll need to pre-dry them before storing them. Freshly harvested seeds have a moisture content of 20% to 40%. The fastest way to remove this excess water is to spread the seeds out in the sun, or in the oven at the lowest setting and with the door open. Spread the drying seeds in a thin layer to provide good air circulation. Use a thermometer to be sure that the temperature stays below 95°F, since higher temperatures can damage seeds. After a few days of initial drying, you can use desiccants to continue the drying process.

We've done several trials to see how fast seeds lose moisture in a sealed jar with a desiccant. In one case, we put three freshly harvested packets of wheat seeds in large containers that also contained an amount of silica gel equal to the weight of the seeds. The seeds had 30% to 40% moisture content when they were put in the containers. During the first eight days, the silica gel had to be removed and redried almost daily because it was absorbing so much moisture from the seeds. After this initial period, it had drawn most of the moisture out of the seeds and did not need to be redried as often. After 30 days, the seeds contained 6% moisture. Drying seeds in a container with a desiccant is good because the seeds dry slowly, which has a more uniform and thorough effect than does rapid drying in hot air.

It's a little messy to handle loose desiccant, so we often put it into paper coin envelopes. We cut a window in each envelope and cover the opening with clear tape so the desiccant's color indicator is visible. Desiccants can also be sealed in small cloth bags. (Remember that moisture passes right through paper and cloth.) Whenever the cobalt chloride changes color from blue to lavender or pink, it's time to redry the desiccant. We usually set the packets on baking pans, dry them in the oven, then replace them in the storage containers.

Desiccant that is saturated with water will dry completely in 16 hours at about 250°F. Don't expose it to higher temperatures, as overheating can damage a desiccant and destroy its moisture-absorbing capacity. At 160°F, the minimum temperature for complete drying, it may take as long as 48 hours to completely regenerate the desiccant. Microwave drying is faster—about 80% of the moisture can be removed from small packets of desiccant after ten minutes in a microwave. But microwave drying appears to be too fast to completely remove the moisture, and desiccant can overheat in a microwave.

These desiccants are fine, granular materials. It's impossible to tell by looking if calcium aluminosilicate clay (upper left) or untreated silica gel (upper right) is dry or saturated. Silica gel treated with a cobalt chloride moisture indicator is blue if dry (bottom left) or pink if saturated (bottom right).

Storing dry seeds

To store seeds that you've harvested and dried, or to save packets of purchased seeds (which were pre-dried before packaging), you need a small amount of desiccant and a moisture-proof container. We put the equivalent of a 1-in. layer of desiccant in the bottom of a gallon jar, then cram the jar full of seed packets. If you're using zip-lock sandwich bags, a teaspoon of desiccant in the bag should keep the contents dry for months. Check the color indicator every few months, and redry the desiccant as needed. A well-sealed container will stay dry for years without renewal.

If you open the container frequently to put seeds in or to take them out, you'll need to redry the desiccant more often. The moisture that enters when you open the container is absorbed by the desiccant, so opening the container does not hurt the seeds. If you keep seed-storage containers in a refrigerator or a freezer, wait a few hours so they can warm up to room temperature before you open them. Moisture from warm air condenses on cool objects—better for it to condense on the outside of the container than on the inside.

Knowing that seeds can be damaged if their moisture content drops too low, we measured the percent of moisture in tomato, radish and wheat seeds that had been stored with a large amount of dry silica gel in a sealed container for five years. The moisture content ranged from 3.4% to 4.6%, but all three groups of seeds had excellent germination—as good after five years of storage as after harvest. The risk of damaging seeds by overdrying them with a desiccant appears to be very small.

There's one caution, though: A few kinds of seeds, notably legumes such as peas, beans or sweet peas, can develop "hard" seed coats at moisture levels below about 6%. Hard seeds are still very much alive, but they go into a state of deep dormancy. It's very difficult to get hard seeds to germinate, so legumes should be air-dried and kept in cold, sealed storage without a desiccant. □

Bruce Bugbee teaches crop physiology at Utah State University in Logan, Utah.

Perennials from Cuttings

A simple, low-cost way to multiply your plants

You can propagate a wide variety of perennials by taking cuttings—portions of stems with leaves—and keeping them in potting mix under moist conditions until they make roots. Clay pots, 5 in. or 6 in. in diameter, are big enough to hold several cuttings from one plant and reduce the risk of overwatering.

by B. J. Morris

Those of us wishing to add to the bounty of our borders are often caught between our dreams and our pocketbooks, but by learning to propagate hardy perennials from cuttings, we can expand our gardens inexpensively. Many perennials can be propagated easily by rooting pieces of stems cut from actively-growing plants. Basically, this technique requires cutting and potting up the stems, and then waiting patiently for a few months for the young plants to make roots and mature for transplanting. (Perennials can also be propagated by root division. See pp. 68-71.)

A stem cutting is a piece of the growing portion of a plant that can be induced, under favorable conditions, to grow roots of its own. A plant grown from a cutting will always be identical to the plant it was taken from. Seed-grown plants can differ considerably from their parents, due to the genetic variability of cross-pollination.

When I started selling hardy perennials from a homemade greenhouse on our family farm 20 years ago, I discovered that the only way to make a profit would be to do as much of my own propagating as possible. The farm, near Seattle, Washington, provided plenty of growing space, an abundant

Photo: Susan Kahn

supply of materials for mulching and fertilizing, and a climate that made it easy to grow a wide variety of hardy perennials. All I had to do was learn how to propagate the plants.

My main sources of information were knowledgeable gardeners, books and personal experience. I discovered—painfully—that the first two sources were not infallible, but the third *was*, as long as I was meticulous about keeping notes and not jumping to conclusions.

Let me walk you through this propagation process, explaining how I do it and sharing my reasons for doing it that way. Once you understand the equipment and the procedure, you can start experimenting on your own, learning what works best for you in your particular situation.

Gardeners have been rooting cuttings for centuries with pretty basic tools. Start with simple equipment and use plants that are easy to work with. Success with these easy plants will encourage you to experiment with more difficult ones. Choose as your first subjects for cuttings those plants that will grow well and easily in your climate. Hold off on investing in expensive equipment until you feel you've mastered the basics; by then you'll know what you want in the way of specialized gadgetry.

Preparing the pots

Clay pots are my choice because they're easy to sterilize and to keep evenly watered. A day or two before taking cuttings, I scrub the pots and run them through the dishwasher. Then I soak them for an hour or so in a disinfectant solution of 1 T. household bleach to 1 gal. of water. I then mix up a sterile medium of one-half commercial, soilless potting mix and one-half perlite.

When the pots are dry, I cover the drain hole in each with a curved piece of broken pot, or potsherd, so that the medium won't wash out when the pots are watered. Then I fill the pots with the medium, leveling it off at the rims. The medium will settle later when the pots are watered.

Next, I set several filled pots in an old roasting pan and pour water around them to a depth of 2 in. I also water the pots gently from the top until the water level in the roasting pan starts to rise, telling me that the pots have taken up as much water as they can hold. (I use an old coffee pot for this—it works a lot better for me than a sprinkling can.) Then I lay a sheet of glass over the tops of the pots to keep things clean, and leave them to soak for a day or so. After the pots are well soaked, I take them out of the roasting pan and set them aside to drain.

Preparing the pots

Before taking cuttings, Morris soaks glass-covered clay pots of medium in 2 in. of water for a day or more.

Taking cuttings—When the pots are ready, I take the cuttings. Hardy fuchsias are a good first-time subject; so are mints, chrysanthemums, phlox (*Phlox paniculata*) and obedient plant (*Physostegia virginiana*). I choose plants that are actively growing and that have not yet started hardening—this stage is known as the half-ripe stage. Taking cuttings works with many hardy perennials, but it won't work with monocotyledonous plants—those whose seeds contain only a single cotyledon, or seed leaf—such as grasses and bulbous plants.

It's important to start cuttings when the stems are at the proper stage of growth. Underripe cuttings usually rot; cuttings that are too mature will root slowly or not at all. When I began propagating plants from cuttings, I chose fairly green, unripe stems and took half a dozen cuttings every week for several weeks, potting each group and watching their development until I learned at what stage of maturity each type of plant rooted best.

Terminal cuttings—Cuttings taken from the tip of the stem usually root better than cuttings taken from farther down. This can present a difficulty: tip cuttings are always less ripe than stem cuttings, but when tip growth is ready, the stem cuttings frequently are too mature to root well. It's sometimes hard to know when tip growth is at just the right stage of maturity for rooting, so I like to take a few cuttings from farther down the stem while I'm at it. This provides me with cuttings at two stages of maturity, increasing the chances that rooting will occur.

To take a cutting, simply sever the desired portion of the stem from the parent plant. (The drawings on pp. 24-25 show the stages of taking cuttings.) I take cuttings 4 in. to 6 in. long, using a very sharp knife to avoid crushing the stem. I like to get six or eight cuttings from a plant, but sometimes there is enough stem for only two or three. It's not a question of harming the plant by taking too many cuttings; rather, it is more a question of aesthetics—taking too many cuttings can spoil the looks of a favorite garden plant for the rest of the season. For the sake of the parent plant, I remove the cutting just above a leaf node. The plant heals better when cut just above a leaf node.

Then I trim the lower end of the cutting just *below* a node, the point where new roots will form. Do this right away, even if you're not quite ready to stick the cuttings in pots. Actively-growing stems contain growth hormones that induce rooting. Once a stem is cut, these hormones start moving toward the cut. If you delay in trimming the cuttings, when you do trim them you may be losing some of the growth hormones.

Hard-to-root cuttings are lacking in those natural hormones. Old-timers used to put an easy-to-root cutting like wandering jew or mint in the same hole with a hard-to-root cutting. A variation on this is willow water, made by crushing willow stems and soaking them in water. This solution is then strained and used to water new cuttings. Gardeners used such homemade hormone treatments before the development of synthetic growth-regulating substances. These commercial rooting hormones are similar to natural growth hormones, stimulating root development on cuttings. Packaged hormones are very useful when you're dealing with hard-to-root subjects.

I carefully remove all the leaves from the bottom half of the cutting, and cut some of the remaining leaves in half crosswise, to reduce the amount of moisture lost through transpiration. When removing foliage, use sharp scissors. I'm always tempted to do it with my thumbnail, but that might damage the stem. Then I wrap the cuttings with a damp paper towel and put them in a plastic bag to keep them from drying out.

Potting up the cuttings—I make holes in the potting medium with a heavy nail or a skinny pencil. The hole should provide a snug fit for the cutting, and it should be a little shorter than the distance from the bottom of the cutting to the first leaf. I like to put the cuttings in a ring about 1 in. from the outer

Propagating half-ripe cuttings of hardy perennials

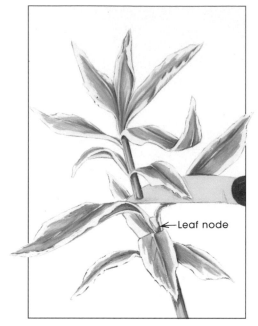

1. Take a cutting *just above a leaf node. This avoids unattractive stem ends and promotes branching on the parent plant. Using a sharp knife to remove cuttings from the parent plant avoids bruising stems.*

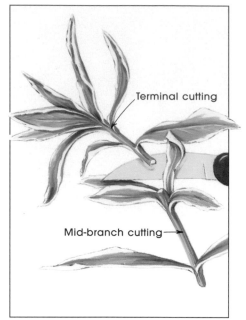

1A. Try taking cuttings *from farther down the stem. Terminal cuttings, from the top of a stem, are less ripe than lower portions of the stem. Additional cuttings will better your chances of success.*

2. Trim *each 4-in. to 6-in. cutting just below a leaf node to induce root growth at the base of the cutting.*

edge of the pot, because some plants root better that way—nobody really knows why, but it's a belief the old-timers hold, and I cling to it.

Insert the cutting carefully, keeping it straight and making sure it doesn't bend or break. The bottom of the cutting should touch the medium because an air space under the cutting will inhibit rooting. Place cuttings far enough apart so that their leaves don't touch. Extras can fill in the space in the center of the pot.

Keeping things straight—As soon as I've potted up the cuttings, I identify them on a 4-in. plant label, recording the name of the plant, where the cutting came from and the date. To avoid confusion, never mix two kinds of cuttings in a pot. I water in the cuttings, using my old coffee pot and getting as little water on the foliage as possible. This settles the medium around the stems. Then I press the medium gently with my fingers, to make doubly sure that the cuttings are firmly settled.

Using a propagating box—Cuttings root best when set on a source of gentle heat (from 70°F to 74°F) and placed under glass to maintain humidity. I have a propagating box made from an old aquarium with 1 in. of fine

gravel in the bottom for drainage. Its cover is a sheet of glass cut from a broken window. I can set the lid slightly ajar to keep things from getting too damp in there if we have a spell of cool, gray weather. It's not fancy, but the price was right, and it works like a charm.

Where you keep the propagating box is important. Placing it on a small electric propagating mat in bright shade is best. These mats create the ideal environment for cuttings, because they provide warmth at the base of pots while the air around the cuttings' foliage stays cooler.

Alternate methods—You can make a less expensive alternative to a propagating mat with a soil heating cable laid in a flat and covered with 2 in. of damp sand. Pots of cuttings can be set right on the sand bed.

Or, you might find a warm enough spot in your home—on top of your refrigerator or hot water heater, for example. To test the area for adequate bottom heat, prepare a pot of cutting mix, dampen it, insert a thermometer and let it sit in your chosen spot for a few days, monitoring the temperature carefully. If the temperature stays between 70°F and 74°F, the spot is a good place to root cuttings. Don't try

to use a household type of heating pad or an electric blanket—these provide too much heat and are not designed to operate safely under wet conditions.

If you're rooting cuttings in a greenhouse, protect them from direct sunlight. A piece of newspaper over the lid of the propagation box works well, or the whole set-up can be kept under the bench. In a greenhouse that has glazing all the way to the ground, place the box near the north or east side to avoid direct afternoon sun.

If I run out of room in my propagating box, I put extra pots of cuttings into plastic bags and insert a couple of thin stakes into each pot to keep the bags from touching the cuttings. I fill the bags with air by blowing into them, and seal them with wire ties. I'm not crazy about this method because it's hard to control the humidity in the bags. Also, some cuttings, especially soft ones, need better ventilation than this method provides.

Keeping records—I keep track of the progress of each batch of cuttings in a notebook. That notebook, with its 20-year history of my progress as a propagator, is one of my richest sources of information. I record the name of the plant, date, number of cuttings, where I got them and anything else that

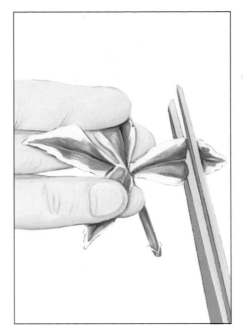

New growth

Mid-branch cutting

3. Carefully remove leaves *from the bottom half of the cutting to reduce water loss through transpiration. Handle cutting by leaves to avoid bruising the stem.*

4. Reduce some remaining leaves *by cutting them in half with scissors. Then insert the cutting into the medium to just below the bottom leaf.*

5. Pot up rooted cuttings *in individual 1-in. pots when they have several sets of new leaves and a healthy root system, as shown.*

seems important. Later on, I record how many of the cuttings succeeded ("struck" is the word plantsmen use), when they were ready to pot up and whatever else occurred that may be helpful the next time I'm propagating that particular type of plant.

Checking the cuttings—If the medium looks dry during the next two weeks, I put the pots back into the roasting pan with 2 in. of water, let them soak until the medium is moist, then allow the pots to drain and return them to the propagating case. Now and then, a cutting will give up the ghost. When that happens, I remove it right away to prevent the development and spread of rot and disease.

After two weeks, I tug very gently on a test cutting to see if it has rooted. If it budges at all, I press it back into place and wait a few more days before checking again. If it tugs back, I know it's rooting and I'll give the cutting a couple more weeks to fully establish roots. Unless I'm in a perishing hurry, I wait until everything in the pot that's going to root has done so before removing any of the new plants to their own pots. To some extent, this depends on what's practical. If the cuttings have been in the propagating box for a long time, and some aren't

rooted, I won't give them a second chance unless the plant I'm trying to propagate is rare or expensive. It also depends on whether there are other pots of cuttings clamoring for space in the box.

Potting up young plants—After the cuttings have rooted, I knock them out of the pot of starting mix, separate them gently and plant them into small, individual pots. I like to use 1-in.-diameter plastic pots for this. Avoid larger

pots because the excess soil tends to become sour and soggy and is an open invitation to disease. Once in individual pots, plants go into a shady place at a temperature between 60°F and 65°F. I gradually move them into brighter light, and repot the young plants into 4-in. pots when roots have filled the 1-in. pots. The length of time plants stay in the 4 in. pots varies depending on temperature, day length and growth habit of the plants, but a month is the minimum time for sufficient root growth. By the time the roots have filled the pot, you will have sturdy plants ready to set outdoors as soon as the conditions are right. Protect newly-set plants from the sun for a few days.

When you succeed at this type of propagation, you may well find yourself the owner of more plants than you know what to do with. You can give them away or trade with friends and neighbors. You can donate special plants to charitable organizations that have plant sales. And if you move to the country to find more space for your growing plant collections, you won't be the first gardener to do so. □

B. J. Morris, a former nursery owner, now gardens for pleasure in Carnation, Washington.

Banded Cuttings

Excluding light stimulates root formation

by Nina Bassuk and Brian Maynard

More and more ornamental trees and shrubs are now propagated vegetatively. That is, a piece of parent plant, frequently a stem cutting, is coaxed to grow into a new plant, and the off-spring and parent are identical in all characters. (Seed-grown plants do not necessarily reproduce the characteristics of the parent.) Stem cuttings from some kinds of trees, notably willows, produce roots quickly and grow into new plants. However, many commonly planted, desirable shade trees, such as maples, oaks and pines, normally are very difficult to root from cuttings. In our research during the past five years, we've focused on the techniques of etiolation and banding as means of rooting these problematic plants more successfully.

Etiolation simply means growing plants in the dark. Typically, we cover dormant plants just before bud burst, and let the new shoots grow out in the dark. These shoots are pale and succulent, and they subsequently produce roots much more easily than do their counterparts grown in the light. We then place an opaque black band around the base of the shoot—a process called banding. When the plant is uncovered, the banded zone remains white and tender, while the rest of the shoot turns green. Later, when we cut off the shoot and root the cutting, roots form in the zone that was covered by the band.

Although our techniques are quite simple, we've observed dramatic improvements in the propagation of a wide variety of difficult-to-root plants. For example, we found that 50% of etiolated, banded cuttings from paperbark maple, *Acer griseum*, produced roots; only 7% of the untreated control cuttings produced roots. For commercial growers, the techniques seem to have potential for reducing the cost and improving the quality of desirable, but previously difficult-to-propagate, trees and shrubs. The techniques, however,

Before uncovering the new, etiolated shoots of these white pines, Bassuk and Maynard added Velcro bands to the intended rooting zone.

A frame supporting black cloth or plastic shades new growth on a section of hedge.

Plastic garbage bags shade individual branches on a tree. Openings at the bottom and top provide ventilation and avoid overheating.

are easily learned by the amateur and provide the means to reproduce an individual plant such as a maple tree that has particularly vivid fall foliage, a favorite shrub in your yard, or an interesting specimen from a friend's garden.

How to do it

Cuttings are most likely to form roots if the parent plant is healthy, and it's easier to propagate from a young, actively growing tree than from an aging specimen that's lost its vigor. If you're patient, it's worthwhile to prune, fertilize and water a tree over one growing season in preparation for making cuttings the next year. Such care is rewarded by a higher percentage of successful rootings. You can make cuttings from plants that are established in the garden, or from plants that are growing in containers in a greenhouse or a cold frame.

Wait for the plants to pass through winter dormancy, and watch for when the buds begin to swell in the spring. Just before the buds start to break, plunge the entire plant or individual branches into darkness. We've tried different methods of covering plants. In the greenhouse, we enclose a bench full of plants in a curtained canopy of densely woven, opaque black fabric. Outdoors, we've built a wooden frame over a hedge to support a layer of black fabric or plastic. You might try covering small plants with cardboard or wooden boxes. It's easiest to shade individual branches with one or two black plastic garbage bags stretched over a wire tomato cage. Leave the bags open at the bottom, and cut a few ventilation slits at the top to prevent overheating. It doesn't have to be pitch-black inside, but the covering should block at least 90% of the light. Peek inside every day or so to inspect the growing shoots. Compared to normal branches growing in the light, the etiolated branches will appear white or pale-colored, tender and succulent, and stretched or elongated between the leaf nodes.

As soon as the stems are long enough to work on without damaging the brittle tips (about 2 in. to 3 in.), we apply bands right at the base of the new growth, the

Photos: Nina Bassuk

intended rooting zone. Earlier researchers used black electricians' tape, aluminum foil, or strips of paper or rubber to form lightproof bands. We thought of an easier way, and use short pieces of black Velcro fastener.

Velcro consists of a pair of surfaces, a hooked side and a fuzzy side, that can be repeatedly joined together or pulled apart. You can buy Velcro by the foot at fabric, hardware or sporting-goods stores, and cut it into short pieces. Usually we use bands about the size of postage stamps, but when we tried larger bands the cuttings rooted over a wider area. Velcro is easy to apply—just sandwich a stem between the hooks and loops, and squeeze firmly to secure the band in place so it won't slide up or down the stem. Unlike tape, which could girdle a growing twig, Velcro will "give" as the stem expands. It doesn't unstick or unwind after a few days, as tape is prone to do, and it can be removed much more easily than can tape. It also allows you to apply rooting hormones during banding. We press the opened Velcro band onto a supply of rooting-hormone powder before we squeeze it in place on the stem. A dusting of powder sticks to the hooks and fuzz of the Velcro, and then is transferred to the stem. Although it isn't an essential step, we find that adding the hormone helps to get rooting under way. (A common brand of hormone is Rootone, sold at garden centers and by mail-order suppliers.)

The banded developing shoots are then gradually exposed to full sunlight. It's important to proceed slowly here—the most common lament we hear from people first trying etiolation is that when they remove the covering, the succulent, tender stems scorch and subsequently die. Without chlorophyll or other pigmentation, etiolated shoots are defenseless against the burning rays of the sun, much as we are during our first visit to a beach. Just as our gradual exposure to the sun lets us tan without burning, gradually exposing etiolated shoots to full sun allows them to turn green without scorching. At first, we open either the side facing north or the bottom of our shade structures, permitting a small amount of light to enter.

SOURCES OF
ROOTING HORMONES

A.M. Leonard, P.O. Box 816, Piqua, OH 45356. (800) 543-8955. Catalog free.

Brighton By-Products, P.O. Box 23, New Brighton, PA 15066. (800) 245-3502. Catalog $5.00.

Charley's Greenhouse Supply, 1569 Memorial Highway, Mt. Vernon, WA 98273. (206) 428-2626. Catalog $2.00.

Over the period of about one week, we then roll back the cover bit by bit, watching as the color flows into the pale shoots. The shoots aren't liable to damage on dark, cloudy days, but be careful to protect them from bright, hot sun. Some common sense is all you need to avoid disaster at this point.

Normally we leave the bands on the stems for four weeks, although they can be left on between two to six weeks or even longer. Then we collect the shoot, cutting just below the band, and remove the Velcro. The banded section of the stem is still etiolated, and often will be swollen or callused, especially when hormones were applied with the band. With certain tree species, such as European hornbeam or paper birch, we've even found that roots form under the band, giving us a rooted shoot before the cutting is taken from the parent plant!

Flexibility is built into every aspect of these techniques. You can try using different kinds of shading materials, leaving the bands on for shorter or longer periods, using narrow or wide bands, and adding or omitting hormone powder. Instead of etiolation and banding, you might try blanching by putting a band on a young stem that has begun its growth in the light. The result of this process is similar to that of etiolation: white, succulent tissues where the shoot has been covered by a band. Blanching works well for several kinds of shrubs and trees, including Bradford pear (*Pyrus calleryana*) and red oak (*Quercus rubra*). It's also a good way to make cuttings of houseplants that never lose their leaves and go dormant. After the band has been in place for a few weeks, check to see if the stem is pale-colored. Leave the band in place until you're ready to cut off the stem and root it.

To standardize our cuttings, we trim them down to between 4 in. and 6 in. long, leaving two or three leaves on each. We dip the bottom, etiolated ends of the cuttings into a dish of hormone powder, then stick them into rooting medium (we combine two parts coarse horticultural perlite with one part sterile peat moss). We root hundreds of cuttings at a time in greenhouse benches, and use an automatic mist system to prevent them from wilting. Once the cuttings have formed roots an inch or so long, we transplant them to individual pots (about 4 in. in diameter) filled with a standard potting soil. We mist them less and less frequently over a week's time, and when they're adjusted to lower levels of humidity, we set the potted plants in a cold frame to continue growing.

To root just a few cuttings, fill a clean pot with moist rooting medium. Use a sprinkling can to apply a solution of Captan fungicide to the soil mix, allowing the excess to drain through, and wait an hour or so for the Captan fumes to evaporate. Now open a hole with a pencil, dip the cutting in rooting hormone, insert the lower half of the cutting into the hole and tamp the soil in place around the stem. If you want to avoid disturbing and transplanting the rooted cuttings, you can stick each cutting in its own pot. Place each pot in a clean, clear plastic bag, using a few sticks of bamboo to keep the plastic from collapsing on the leaves. Inflate the bag as you'd blow up a balloon and secure the top with a twist-tie. Put the bagged pot in a warm, bright place, but not in direct sun where it would overheat. Open the bag after a few weeks to check the cutting's progress. If roots have formed, you'll feel resistance when you tug gently at the stem. When you're sure that the cutting has developed a root system, begin to harden it off by leaving the top of the bag open. Roll the bag down farther each day, and after a week you can take it off altogether and set the new plant outdoors.

We've noticed that after they have formed roots, cuttings from some trees begin to produce new top growth. Our stewartias (*Stewartia pseudocamellia*), for example, have grown to 2 ft. tall by late summer from cuttings taken in May. However, cuttings from other trees, such as sugar maple (*Acer saccharum*), will form a good root ball and then drop their leaves and go dormant. Whether a plant continues to grow throughout the summer after the cutting is rooted, or whether it roots and then goes dormant for the rest of the year, the new plant can be expected to grow normally in the second and following years.

Even if they're propagated from sturdy trees that are tolerant of sun, wind and cold, small plants growing in containers need protection from these extreme conditions. In the summer, water frequently enough that the young plants don't wilt on hot, dry days. You might place the pots under a tree or on a patio where the plants will be shaded from midday sun. In the winter, sink the pots into the ground and heap mulch over the pots and plants, or set the pots in a cold frame, an unheated garage, or a cellar area where temperatures don't fall much below freezing. The year after rooting the cuttings, you can transplant the young plants to their permanent location.

How it works

Excluding light from shoots is not a new propagation technique. Some of the most common cloning methods—layering, stooling, air-layering and cutting—all involve keeping light from the part of the plant intended to form roots. When air-layering *Ficus*, for example, propagators wrap sphagnum moss around the stem not only to maintain moisture but also to exclude light. Burying raspberry shoots when tip-layering also keeps light out. Stooling apple rootstocks involves placing soil over new growth as it develops. Even in cutting propagation, propagators exclude light by placing the cutting's rooting zone in an opaque medium. Like these other techniques, etiolation and banding are ways to exclude light.

In our research, we examine normal and etiolated stems, trying to understand how the differences between them affect root formation. Etiolation seems to increase the stem's sensitivity to auxin, a plant hormone that can stimulate undifferentiated cells in a stem to develop into a new root system. (Auxin is produced naturally in the tips of growing stems; synthetic auxins are the active ingredient in rooting-hormone powders.) Light seems to inhibit a stem's sensitivity to auxin, darkness to increase it. In addition, etiolated stems contain softer, undifferentiated tissue with less fiber and lignin content, making it easier for the roots to grow out through the stem.

Banding preserves the pale, succulent, immature nature of the etiolated tissue. Even after the rest of the shoot turns green and hardens up, the banded area retains the potential for successful rooting. Unlike the smooth surfaces of foil or tape, Velcro's hooks will wound or scarify tender stem tissue, which increases the stem's rooting potential by stimulating a proliferation of callus cells. Some of these cells develop into the root initials that emerge through scars, nodes or the cut end of the stem. Others form the connection between the new roots and the existing xylem, or water-transport system.

We're continuing to develop these techniques and to apply them to different kinds of plants. So far we've tested more than 40 types of trees and shrubs. For each new plant, we try all possible combinations of treatments and compare the response to the results obtained with untreated cuttings. We've tried etiolation plus banding, just banding (i.e., blanching), banding plus hormone, and other variations of the technique, and we find that one combination is often more effective than others, depending on which plant species is being tested. At the same time, as we investigate the physical and chemical differences between stems grown in the light and stems grown in the dark, we're helping to explain the fascinating process of how stems form roots and grow into new plants. □

Dr. Nina Bassuk is associate professor and program leader of urban horticulture at Cornell University in Ithaca, New York. Brian Maynard is a graduate student in floriculture and ornamental horticulture at Cornell.

Protected by the Velcro, part of the stem of this European hornbeam remains white.

To root the etiolated and banded stem, first trim off the top, leaving two or three leaves above the etiolated zone.

Wet the bottom end of the cutting, then dip it in rooting-hormone powder. Insert the cut stem halfway into a hole in moist, coarse-textured rooting medium and tamp the soil in place around the stem.

Form a tent around the pot with bamboo and a plastic bag, inflating the bag to hold the plastic away from the soil and leaves.

In three months since the cutting was taken, this European hornbeam has grown several new leaves and a root system that fills the pot.

Photos: Staff

Shopping for the Best Perennials

Learn how they've been grown

Editor's note: Decades ago, nearly all perennial plants were grown in small local nursery fields. They were dug, usually in the spring, and sold directly to nearby garden centers or gardeners. Nowadays, millions of perennial plants start life in the fields of large wholesale nurseries. But about the same time as apples are harvested, a majority of the perennials—as many as can stand the treatment—are dug, divided, trimmed, cleaned and packed. And like apples, the plants are stored at near-freezing temperatures in giant refrigerated warehouses. In the spring, most of the plants are shipped to retail nurseries that pot them up and sell them as soon as possible. The rest, still dormant, are sold directly to gardeners, by mail-order and at garden centers.

This is an expedient way to produce and sell perennials, but it isn't necessarily the best way. The plants are often relatively small and weak. If you simply *must* have a particular variety of something, and your only choice is to buy a dormant or newly potted division, then take what you can get. The germplasm is there, even if the only specimen you can buy is a puny example.

Yet if you're shopping for any of the common, and many of the not-so-common, perennials, why settle for less than the healthiest, hardiest, most robust specimens? Experienced gardeners go out of their way to obtain the best nursery stock they can buy (which, by the way, isn't always the most expensive).

To help you decide what to look for, we asked two nursery owners to describe how they grow the perennials they sell, and to explain why they think their methods produce the best plants. Elisabeth Sheldon maintains that plants grown in outdoor nursery beds, and transplanted with a generous root ball, have outstanding size, vigor and hardiness. Diane Erickson Schneider points out that container-grown plants are easy on the gardener and nearly foolproof to transplant.

FIELD-GROWN PLANTS

by Elisabeth Sheldon

Last spring I closed down a small perennial-plant business that I'd been running for ten years. I must say it's a great relief, for I conducted business the hard way. Not only did I do much of the work myself, helped by a young woman only three days a week, but I grew most of the plants in the ground. The only ones I grew and sold in pots were those that resent having their roots disturbed—poppies, for example, or gypsophilas, platycodons, flax or columbines.

Growing plants in the field or in raised beds meant we had to cultivate, hoe, weed and water a large area. We mulched wherever we could with thick layers of straw. That worked well in the summer when we wanted to keep moisture in and weeds out, but we had to pull the straw away from the plants in early spring, as it kept the ground too cold and wet and prevented the plants from making early growth—or any growth at all in some cases.

Most tiring of all was the heavy work of digging, wrapping and carrying every plant we sold. I never weighed an helenium, goatsbeard or Japanese iris with its accompanying ball of earth, but each clump must have weighed 30 lb. or more. Then, of course, we had to refill the holes with new soil mixed with peat, manure and grit.

You might wonder why I put myself to so much trouble,

(Text continues on p. 30.)

CONTAINER-GROWN PLANTS

by Diane Erickson Schneider

My husband and I operate a wholesale perennial nursery. Every year we grow 200,000 plants of 250 varieties, which we sell to garden centers and landscapers. We grow all our perennials in containers because we're convinced that it's best for the plants and best for our customers. Container growing means we can control light, moisture, fertilizer, pests, diseases and effects of the weather. Container-grown perennials are convenient to transport and nearly foolproof to transplant, and they can be set out any time from spring through fall. I'll describe our container production techniques, as well as the reasons behind them.

Production starts when we pot a new crop of seedlings, cuttings and divisions in the summer. Our plants get well established and grow to full size in their pots during the warm weather. After going dormant in the fall, they spend the winter in insulated but unheated greenhouses. When we sell them the next spring, they'll bloom the same year.

We use 3½-in.-wide by 4-in.-deep plastic pots for the majority of the plants, and 5½-in.-wide by 6-in.-deep pots for extremely vigorous perennials or ones propagated by division. A 4-in. pot is large enough to allow most perennials' roots and shoots to develop fully, yet small enough to be economical for the consumer. We use black

(Text continues on p. 31.)

(Text continued from p. 29.)

when it would seem more practical to grow everything in containers. With container growing, there's no hoeing or cultivating and very little weeding to do. The pots can easily be watered with a hose or even an automatic sprinkler system. (Of course, I could just as well have had a sprinkler system in my nursery area.) It isn't necessary to replace topsoil that's been sold, and it's quite a lot easier to hand people plants in pots than to trundle around with a wheelbarrow and a spade, digging specimens out of nursery beds. Another advantage is that customers can take their time about getting their purchases into the ground; it won't hurt the plants to sit around in their pots for days or weeks longer—they're used to it.

So why did I do it the hard way? Was it just a case of being old-fashioned and loath to change? Was it that I didn't want to mar the looks of my garden with the plastic greenhouses necessary to protect container-grown plants through the winter? Partly the former. Certainly the latter. But as the years went by and the going got rougher, I might have capitulated to more "modern" methods if I hadn't made some observations as I went along.

The first was that most perennials dislike pots. You can keep them alive in pots, but they don't really thrive—and why should they? They want to send their roots down and into the earth, foraging for nourishment. You can douse them with plant food so they'll have a healthy appearance, but it's mostly just that—appearance. Further, when they're kept in a greenhouse or tunnel for protection from wind, sun and the severe trials of winter, they don't have to develop the fortitude it takes to face the elements.

Add to all this the fact that most container plants are grown in Pro-Mix or some other concoction of peat, perlite, milled sphagnum and other fluffy substances. When transplanted into the ground, their roots recoil in horror from actual soil containing clay, rocks or other material that requires determination to penetrate or circumvent. Instead of reaching out into the real world, they continue to go round and round in their fake soil mixture all summer. The result is that, while such plants may seem to be doing well during the mild weather, they often can't hack it through the winter.

When plants are potted in a combination of Pro-Mix and real garden soil and lined up outdoors, rather than indoors, they do much better; but even then they don't make the growth they would if they were planted in the ground. I conducted an experiment one summer with several perennials—potentillas, coralbells and campanulas. I raised them from seed, then pricked them out of their flats, first into 2½-in. and later into 4-in. pots. When it came time to move them from the 4-in. pots, I planted half of each lot into raised nursery beds and half into larger pots, using as a medium a combination of garden soil and Pro-Mix, to which I added bone meal.

A month later it was hard to believe that the plants were

Elisabeth Sheldon grew perennials in raised nursery beds. When a customer bought a plant, she would dig it carefully and wrap the root ball. Plants grown this way are large, vigorous and hardy.

"The plants in raised beds were easily three times as big as the potted ones."

siblings. The plants in raised beds were easily three times as big as the ones that simply had been repotted. Both groups had been outdoors and had had plenty of sunlight and water. The only difference in their treatment, apart from the potted plants' growing in a special mix, was that the plants in the raised beds had had all the root room they wanted.

I'm convinced that the difference in size and vigor of perennials grown in the ground, compared to those raised in pots, is maintained when they're sold and transplanted. Many serious gardeners agree, and they're willing to drive extra miles and pay more to get field-grown plants. My prices were higher than those of my local competitors (one of whom was right across the road), but I was able to stay in business because of the quality and staying power of my plants.

When I dug plants to sell, I swathed them in wet newspaper or put them in recycled plastic bags from the grocery store. My customers had to keep them cool, moist and shaded until they were ready to plant them—ideally immediately, or at most within a few days. If the weather was cool, gray and moist, the gardener's job was then finished. But under warm, bright, dry conditions, I advised customers to "puddle-in" the plants—that is, to fill each planting hole with water and let it soak in, set the plant in place and gently press loose earth around it, then add more water. I also recommended covering the transplant with an inverted basket, fiber pot or similar shelter to protect it from sun and wind for a few days, until the hair roots had begun to bring in moisture again. The cover had to be removed at night. Now, this procedure, admittedly, involves a certain amount of trouble. You have to remember to cover the plants in the morning before you leave for work—if you leave for work—and to uncover them at dinner time or later. If it rains while you're gone, you'll be upset as you think of your plants huddled under their covers, unable to take advantage of the shower. Of course, if you're the happy-go-lucky type, you'll ignore instructions and won't cover the plants at all and they might just survive. Some healthy perennials, even when moved in midsummer with no subsequent protection provided, will put up new growth after the leaves they were moved with have shriveled away.

Those who say that container-grown plants are easier to move really mean that they're more convenient. If they've been sitting outdoors, and if they're not pot-bound, you won't even have to protect them from the sun and wind after transplanting. If the roots of the potted plant are a tangled mass, however, you'll have to loosen them so they'll travel down and out—in which case the plant will need as much protection as if it had been dug. So there you go. ☐

Elisabeth Sheldon operated Ridge House Garden in Lansing, New York.

Photo: George Sheldon

(Text continued from p. 29.)

plastic pots because black allows very little light transmission, and roots develop best in the dark.

The critical part of growing perennials is developing vigorous, healthy root systems. Soil mix and fertilizer play important roles. We use a custom-blended soil mix made of peat moss, vermiculite and perlite. These components offer a nearly sterile growing medium with good aeration and water retention. The mix has little nutritional value, but it has the capacity to grab onto and then release supplied nutrients. We provide a balanced liquid fertilizer plus trace elements at each watering, adjust the irrigation water to a pH of 5.0 to 5.5 (optimum for nutrient uptake in a peat-based mix) and use professional lab services to monitor soil nutrient levels throughout the growing season.

Container growing is high-density growing. Each of our eight 20-ft. by 96-ft. greenhouses holds nearly 20,000 of the 4-in. pots, tucked "pot tight" throughout production. Here we can create the microenvironments that result in high-quality plants.

In the summer, we cover the greenhouses with shade cloth. Plants are organized by the degree of shade they prefer—33%, 47% or 55%. Full-sun lovers go in an uncovered growing area. The shade cloth also acts as windbreak, bug screen, and protection from hail and light frost. We can change the cloth on a house in less than 15 minutes, so it's easy to maximize light conditions as daylength or weather changes. In the winter, we remove the shade cloth and cover the structures with a double layer of plastic; clear on the inside, opaque white on the outside. The white plastic reflects light to help keep the greenhouses from overheating on sunny winter days.

Not all growers overwinter, or "vernalize," perennials, but we do, since this conditions the plants to bloom. The crucial factor in overwintering is making sure that the soil temperature doesn't fluctuate widely. We set the perennials in flats directly on the ground in the greenhouse, and cover them with ¼-in.-thick sheets of white, breathable, insulating foam, which works just like an insulating layer of snow. Soil temperature stays at a steady 24° to 35°F, even though air temperature in the greenhouse varies from -10° to 50°F.

We remove the foam in March when the soil in the pots has thawed and there are signs of new shoot growth, but we leave the covering on the houses for several more weeks so the plants can adjust slowly to increased light levels under continued cool temperatures. As the chance of frost decreases, we cut off the white plastic, leaving only the clear underlayer. Now the plants begin to experience the greenhouse effect, but we open the oversize greenhouse doors to provide good ventilation. Our goal is to bring the plants out of dormancy slowly and to grow them cool. We want the new growth to be green but somewhat "hard"-

Diane Schneider grows perennials in containers in unheated greenhouses, with careful attention to soil, water, nutrients, light and temperature. She emphasizes the importance of developing a good root system. Plants grown this way are convenient to transport and easy to transplant.

looking, not soft and lush. With healthy root systems already well established, these are plants that will transplant successfully in early spring.

Before closing, I'd like to comment on some of the other ways that perennials are sold. Some perennial growers sell small, bare-root divisions. Before I entered this profession, I used to buy these—and had substantial losses. Now that I've been producing perennials in containers and using them in my own garden, I definitely feel that home gardeners are better off buying larger, rooted, actively growing perennials than any kind of small or dormant material.

Finally, a container alone doesn't guarantee a top-quality plant. There are two types of widely-practiced "container" production that I strongly reject. I call them pseudo-container growing, because neither method concerns itself with the development of the plant's root system.

The first method is to force plants from divisions by growing them in heated greenhouses. Bleeding-hearts, lilies-of-the-valley and hostas are frequently treated this way. Nurseries and garden centers buy dormant divisions and pot them up in February or March, then keep them at temperatures between 50° and 70°F until enough shoot growth appears to make the plants salable. These plants may *look* lush, but in nearly all cases they will have very poor root systems and will not transplant well. Remember, it's the roots that count at transplanting time. Before buying a plant, carefully tip it out of its pot to check the roots. Reject it if its roots are poor, no matter how great the top looks.

The second method is even worse, in my opinion. It consists of digging field-grown plants and stuffing them into pots just before shipping them to the retailer. Unless these plants are sold and planted within a few days, their chances of flourishing are slim. First, digging severs the majority of a plant's root system. Second, in pots, unamended field soil compacts readily and loses its aeration; the higher the clay content, the more rapidly this occurs. It's easy to spot these plants on the retailer's display— they're the sad, droopy ones that wilt even when the soil is wet. Perennials subjected to this treatment take weeks or months to recover in the garden, if indeed they ever do.

I believe that our method of containerized growing results in the highest-quality perennials. The transplanting success rate is high; the plants also hold well in the pots. Some customers use the plants in our large-size containers as specimens on their patios for weeks before transferring them to their perennial borders. We may start producing plants in even larger pots just for this purpose. ☐

"Container-grown perennials are convenient and nearly foolproof to transplant."

Diane Erickson Schneider and her husband, Lee, live in Acton, Ontario.

A matted clump of roots and old soil show that the andromeda held by the author was recently moved to the large container after staying too long in the previous container. Knowing how to examine the top growth and roots in the nursery can help you buy healthy plants.

Photos, these two pages: Chris Curless

How to Shop for Shrubs and Trees

A buyer's guide to picking healthy plants

by Nancy Carney

When you go to a nursery to buy a shrub or tree, what you're looking for is a plant that will grow quickly yet sturdily, make steady progress and endure. What you don't want is a plant that will cling to life for a season or two, die and have to be replaced.

In over 30 years of buying nursery plants for my garden, I've discovered some dependable methods for selecting healthy plants, and I'll share them here. I'll tell you how to examine leaves, branches, stems and roots for signs of health, and I'll describe tests for determining vigor. A word of caution: you'll have to handle the plants and look at their roots. As long as you're careful, you won't harm the plants, but if you're worried about damage or uncertain about the nursery's reaction, ask for permission or help.

Know the nursery

Well-run nurseries tend to have healthy plants. There are several ways to identify good nurseries. Ask your gardening friends which nurseries they use, and try places with good reputations. When you visit a nursery, check for knowledgeable salespeople. Research the plants you want to buy and then quiz the nursery's staff to see if they can answer your questions. The best nurseries will have a good return policy. Most will require you to save your receipts and return plants within a limited time period for refund or replacement. Guaranteed plants are more expensive, but cost less than having an unguaranteed plant die and then buying a replacement.

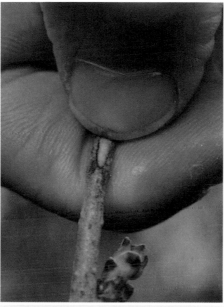

Scraping the bark reveals green, living tissue on a lilac branch. When plants are leafless, a look beneath the bark can reveal if a branch is dormant or dead.

The way plants are handled at the nursery affects their health. Shade-loving plants should be protected from the sun. Sun-lovers shouldn't bake or wilt. And plant roots should never dry out. If a plant feels light for its size when you pick it up, the soil may be too dry. (Always lift a plant by its container or root ball. Picking a plant up by the trunk can damage the trunk, tear the roots or create air pockets in the root ball.)

Signs of health

A good look at the top of a shrub or tree will tell you a lot about its health. A plant that looks wilted, seems short on leaves or branches, or has discolored leaves is probably sick. Each leaf should be firm but pliable. You can feel leaves of the same species or similar plants in the garden to get an idea of how pliable healthy leaves should be.

Look among the plant's branches for new growth—soft, green tissue with tiny new leaves. If you can examine a similar plant established in a well-cared-for garden, compare it to the nursery plant. The new growth on the two plants should be similar—the new stems should be the same thickness and the new leaves should be about the same size and spaced at equal distances along the branches. If the nursery plant's leaves are smaller or farther apart or if the stems are more spindly, the plant is probably not receiving adequate care.

Look for good foliage color. It should be uniform throughout the entire plant, except for new growth. Yellow color or brown edges or tips indicate root damage from improper watering or fertilizing. If whole branches (or the entire plant) droop, the plant may be dry, overfertilized or too exposed. When shopping at the end of the season, be wary of premature fall color. Early dormancy suggests poor summer care.

The shape of a plant is an indication of its health. The branching should be balanced on all sides of the plant, and the foliage, if present, should be full. If your potential purchase is a suckering shrub—a plant that makes new stems from the base or the roots—check for new shoots at the soil line. They should be similar in size to those already growing above ground. Make sure upright trees, such as pine and spruce, have a trunk with a healthy tip—a leader. If the leader is dead, it's hard to grow a straight tree, though you can encourage a new leader by training a top branch vertically.

If you're looking at deciduous shrubs and trees in early spring or late fall, when they're leafless, you

The roots of a root-bound daphne twist around themselves, a condition that will later lead to strangling. The darker-colored roots that were above the soil line provide the clue.

(Left) The top of the pine tree has grown out of proportion to its small container. (Above) Removing the pot reveals that the root system is so overgrown that little soil remains.

can check if a plant is dormant or dead by scraping a small patch of bark off a branch. (See photo on p. 33.) If the branch is alive, you should see moisture beneath the bark, and the color of the exposed area should be faintly green. If the color beneath the bark is gray or a dull beige, the branch is probably dead. Sometimes plants suffer transplant shock, which kills a few branches but not the whole plant. So if your first scrape turns up dead wood, scrape other branches, moving closer to the root system each time to see how far the damage extends.

Before you buy, check trees and shrubs for diseases and insects. The plant's foliage and stems should be absolutely free of insects and disease. Check for holes and other signs of trouble. Look at the undersides of leaves and along the growing tips first, then check the branches. Mites spin fine webs on the undersides of leaves, which often show mottled yellow upper surfaces as well. If leaves have black blotches, red or yellow spots, or holes surrounded by a discoloration, a rust or other fungal disease is present. If you see light-colored little bumps on the branches, they are probably scale, immobile sap-sucking insects.

What roots say

Nurseries sell shrubs and trees in containers or "B&B"—balled-and-burlapped (their roots and a small amount of soil are wrapped in burlap and tied). Both container and balled-and-burlapped plants are fine, but you must evaluate their health differently.

Container-grown plants—Container shrubs and trees have one potential advantage—treated properly, their roots are never disturbed. If protected by a container, roots can't be jarred, bumped or broken when the plant is moved. The roots remain intact when the young plants outgrow their original containers, because the entire root ball is dropped into a larger container. This protection is particularly important for plants with roots that are easily damaged by transplanting, such as trees with taproots and rhododendrons, which have shallow roots.

The challenge in buying a container-grown plant is to find a healthy root system when you can't see it, but there are signs you can look for. The roots should fill the container without being crowded. If a plant has too many roots for the size of its container, nurserymen say it's root-bound, an

Photos, this page: Mark Kane

unhealthy condition. You can unpot and untangle the roots before planting, but untangling roots defeats the purpose of buying a container-grown plant because it disturbs the roots and can damage them. And while suckering shrubs usually can survive such treatment, many trees and shrubs, such as azaleas and rhododendrons, usually cannot. If you buy a plant with fibrous roots—thin and multi-branched—and discover it is root-bound, slice into the root ball almost to the trunk at 6-in. intervals all around its circumference. As you plant the root ball, pull these cuts open and force soil into them to encourage the plant to send new roots into the surrounding soil.

One way to check if a plant was root-bound is to examine the soil line for evidence that it was grown in a small pot and then set in a container that is much larger. If the original pot was fiber, it may be in the larger pot; you'll find a ring of fiber at the soil line. If there is no fiber pot, you can check for soils of different consistencies or soil that is more matted with roots at the center of the pot than at the outside edges. (See photo on p. 32.)

You can also make an educated guess about the root health of a container-grown plant by examining its top growth. The trunk or stems should be supple above the soil but not wobbly. If you grasp a sapling or young shrub near its base and move it, the stem or trunk should bend above ground, but stay firmly rooted at the ground level. If wobbling the stem creates a hole in the soil at the base of the plant, the plant probably is not well rooted. Try bending similar plants growing in the garden until you develop a feel for the amount of flexibility a trunk should have near ground level.

You can also check roots by poking at the soil in the container. They'll vary in appearance from species to species, but in general the roots should be firm, have an earthy odor and branch out into finer feeder roots. Healthy roots are usually lighter colored than the potting soil. They shouldn't look dark, have a foul smell or feel mushy. If you can't locate surface roots by poking into the soil with your finger, the plant may still be healthy, especially if it's firmly anchored in the container.

Balled-and-burlapped plants—Balled-and-burlapped plants are grown in the ground and are usually lifted every year and root-pruned. When it is time

Unwrapping the burlap covering of this root ball reveals cracks in the soil, indicating damaged roots caused by rough handling.

for them to be sold, they are dug up with a good amount of earth attached to the roots and wrapped in burlap. Because of the annual root-pruning, balled-and-burlapped plants develop a compact root system with lots of feeder roots. They aren't root-bound, so they're more likely to transplant successfully than root-bound container-grown plants. But the labor of digging and pruning makes balled-and-burlapped plants more expensive. They are also more vulnerable to drying out than container-grown plants because much more of the root system is exposed to the air. If they do dry out, resulting root damage leads to poor growth, dieback and leaf loss. Afflicted plants can die after transplanting.

Conduct the same tests for root health in balled-and-burlapped plants as for container-grown plants. The soil used for balled-and-burlapped plants contains more clay than container medium—clay adheres to the feeder roots, helping to hold the root ball together. It also makes the root ball harder to probe and will make the plant heavier to lift. Moving the major stems should move the entire root ball. If it

doesn't, the roots may be damaged. (See photo above.) Knead the ball to make sure it is firm and that it has no lumps of dirt without roots in them.

If a balled-and-burlapped plant is well cared for, a season or two in a nursery won't hurt it. The longer it remains balled and burlapped, the more feeder roots it will grow. The resulting vigorous root system and dense root ball will be easier to transport without damage. The plant will begin to grow vigorously when it is finally reset into soil.

Trust what the leaves, stems and roots tell you. Check the top growth first. Then examine the roots, because if the roots aren't healthy, the plant will have a tough time adjusting. As long as a plant you like passes these health tests, go ahead and buy it, no matter how awkwardly shaped or downtrodden it otherwise appears. You may be pleased to see how well it will respond to your care. ∎

Nancy Carney lectures about gardening and designs gardens when she's not tending her own in Newtown, Connecticut.

A Better Way to Plant Shrubs and Trees

For starters, dig a shallow hole and avoid soil amendments

by Carl Whitcomb

How you plant a shrub or tree determines whether the plant struggles to grow, dies outright, or takes off and thrives. I know this firsthand. For 20 years I conducted research with a wide variety of ornamental shrubs and trees, planting them in different ways and observing the results. I learned, often to my surprise, that many common recommendations about planting are wrong or useless. You may think that the traditional approach to transplanting—digging a deep planting hole, amending the soil with organic matter, pruning branches to compensate for lost roots, and not fertilizing at planting time produces good results, but my research shows that a different approach works better.

Whether you're planting a bare-root, balled and burlapped (B&B), or container plant, your shrub or tree is more likely to thrive if you provide a well-drained site, a wide, shallow planting hole, the right kind and amount of fertilizer, and regular watering. It will do even better if you use organic matter as a mulch instead of as a soil amendment and leave the plant unpruned, unless it has weak, damaged or ill-placed branches.

The time of year is another important consideration when you plant a tree or shrub. Spring, summer and fall

Two inches of shredded bark mulch and a thorough soaking complete the process of planting an evergreen holly. For healthiest growth, shrubs and trees should be planted in wide, shallow holes, provided with good drainage, fertilized if needed, and left unpruned.

can all be appropriate planting times, as long as you take into account the impact of each season on plant growth. In many parts of the country, the cool weather, high humidity, and abundant rainfall of spring make this a particularly good time to plant. In summer, warmer temperatures promote growth but also increase a plant's demand for water, so if you decide to plant at this time, choose a plant that has been well-watered at the garden center, and irrigate it as needed after planting. Fall planting also has advantages—cooler air temperatures reduce the demand for

water while the lingering warmth of the soil encourages rapid root growth. Take care, however, to allow your transplant enough time to become established before winter sets in.

Evaluate the drainage

Check the soil drainage before you plant. No amount of care in planting can make a shrub or tree thrive if the soil is so wet that the roots don't get enough oxygen and they suffocate. To test drainage, dig a hole 8 in. wide and 12 in. deep, fill it with water several times during the day until the soil is saturated and then fill it again in the evening. (See drawing on pp. 38-39.) If there is standing water in the hole 24 hours later, you must improve the drainage or limit yourself to the relatively few woody plants that tolerate wet sites.

The easiest way to improve drainage is to plant on berms or raised mounds of soil. Start by loosening the soil beneath the mound to a depth of 4 in. to 6 in. Next, pile additional topsoil 6 in. to 1 ft. high in a circle at least three times as wide as the root system of the plant, and set it in place as if the top of the mound were ground level. Mounds tend to dry quickly (and the lighter the soil, the faster they dry out), so you have to water diligently the first, and often the second year, until the roots establish themselves.

The surest way to improve drainage is to run perforated drain pipe through a gravel-filled, underground trench.

The pipe must run to a low spot to carry away water. Since most roots are in the top 1 ft. of soil, the pipe must be installed 16 in. to 18 in. deep.

If you can't improve the drainage, plant shrub or tree species that tolerate wet sites. For help in choosing a suitable plant, check with a local nursery or consult these books: *Landscape Plants for Eastern North America*, by Harrison L. Flint ($69.95 ppd., John Wiley & Sons, 1 Wiley Drive, Somerset, NJ 08875); *Pocket Guide to Choosing Woody Ornamentals* by Gerd Krüssmann ($15.95 ppd., Timber Press, 9999 S.W. Wilshire, Portland, OR 97225); and *Know It and Grow It II: A Guide to the Identification and Use of Landscape Plants*, by Carl Whitcomb ($38.00 ppd., Lacebark, Inc., P.O. Box 2383, Stillwater, OK 74076).

Dig a wide planting hole

The ideal planting hole is wide and shallow—at least twice the width of the root system of the plant, and the wider the better. Roots need oxygen for growth, and they get most of it from open spaces between particles of soil. A broad circle of loosened soil around a new shrub or tree helps to insure that the roots have the air they need during the first growing season.

Dig a planting hole the same depth as the root system of your shrub or tree. Deeper holes can lead to trouble. The soil may settle enough after transplanting to create a depression around the plant. If rain collects and stands in this depression, or if soil washes in and packs around the trunk, there is a danger of encouraging root and trunk diseases. Many publications suggest digging a deep planting hole, then packing the soil in the bottom to prevent settling. Since air is vital to root growth, it makes no sense to dig the soil out, then pack it back in.

Prune sparingly, if at all

On the face of it, pruning a shrub or tree at planting time sounds plausible. When a nursery digs up a bare-root or a B&B plant, most of the root system remains in the ground, producing a plant with a top too big for its roots. Even container-grown plants can end up disproportionately top-heavy after their potbound roots are pruned away.

It would seem that such extensive root loss would prevent the plant from taking up enough water, so you'd need to cut back the top to reduce its water needs. But, in fact, my research shows that even if shrubs or trees lose many roots during transplanting, the unpruned plants do better than the pruned ones during the first year. They put on more growth, and fewer of them die. After

two years, the pruned trees catch up with their unpruned neighbors, but pruning takes its toll. The pruned trees, especially those with one-third or more of their branches removed, often have less attractive shapes. Also, severe pruning frequently prompts young trees to produce new branches that are too close to adjacent ones, or that grow out from the trunk at narrow angles. By contrast, unpruned trees generally have better-spaced branches with stronger angles, and they look more natural.

Why does an unpruned shrub or tree thrive? I have a theory. The root system, though diminished in size by digging or pruning, appears to be able to keep up with the early demand for water from the top if the soil has plen-

These two silver maples were the same size and age when planted two years before this photograph was taken. The tree on the left was planted in amended soil containing 20% pine bark, which restricted its growth. The tree on the right was planted without amendments. Since the leaf size and color of both trees are similar, there would be no visual symptoms of the pine bark's effect without the larger tree as a comparison.

ty of moisture. Meanwhile, the root system of an unpruned plant grows faster than that of a pruned plant because expanding leaf buds produce hormones and sugars that stimulate root growth, and the more buds, the faster the growth. Plants with better root systems are more likely to thrive, especially during hot, dry weather.

While I've found that pruning for balance between top and roots does no good, corrective pruning does have a place at planting time. If a shrub or tree has a cluster of branches growing too close together for good looks or health, remove a branch or two. You also should remove damaged branches; the weaker of two branches that cross; and branches that ascend from the trunk at a steep angle, because their crotches,

the places where the branches meet the trunk, will always be weak.

Hold the soil amendments

For decades, gardeners have mixed organic amendments into the soil to help establish newly-planted shrubs and trees. The resulting "lighter" soil might sound like a good idea, but I've found that soil amended with peat moss, pine bark and similar organic materials produces no better results than unamended soil and sometimes gives less vigorous growth. Of all of my findings, this one has generated the most controversy among professionals and home gardeners alike. When I finished my first talk about these experiments, the moderator implied that my results were somehow unpatriotic, commenting that he didn't intend to ask me what I thought about apple pie or motherhood. Actually, I, too, once believed in the need for soil amendments. In fact, my first experiments were designed to learn which additives were best for planting, and I was as surprised as anyone to learn that none of them produced better results than unamended soil. I've since repeated my experiments in several parts of the country and on different kinds of soil, and got the same results.

In the first year or two after planting, the difference between shrubs and trees in amended soil and unamended soil is moderate above ground, but often striking below ground. Since plants in amended soil rarely show visible signs of stress, there is no reason to question the practice. But after digging up hundreds of plants, I've learned that plants in unamended soil send roots as far as 3 ft. or 4 ft. from the original root ball in a year or two, while the roots of plants in amended soil are still largely confined to the planting hole.

Roots in amended soil grow more slowly because they often have too little or too much water. On well-drained sites, soil amendments such as peat often deprive the roots of moisture. The amended soil quickly loses much of the water it absorbs to the surrounding, often finer-textured, soil, which acts like an ink-blotter and pulls water from the peat by capillary action. The loss is very rapid when the ground is relatively dry, and is compounded by the demand for water from the top growth of the plant. During hot, dry spells, when a plant loses lots of water, the amended soil may be dry enough to cause plant stress even though the surrounding unamended soil is still moist enough to support growth.

On poorly-drained sites, soil amendments can collect too much water. The amended soil has a coarser texture than the surrounding soil and therefore allows water to penetrate more rapidly. During a rainy period or prolonged irrigation, the planting hole can fill up like a bathtub, causing roots to suffocate, or suffer enough stress and dieback to encourage root diseases.

Some acid-loving plants, such as azaleas, do grow better when the soil is heavily amended with organic matter, which tends to be acidic as it breaks down. The benefit, however, stems largely from the decrease in soil pH rather than improved soil structure. You could skip the peat moss, lower the pH with powdered or granular sulfur and have equally good results.

If you have organic matter available, you'll have better results if you use it as a mulch, imitating the way organic matter would be added to the soil in nature, rather than using it as a soil amendment.

Fertilize as needed

Should you fertilize newly-planted shrubs and trees? Yes, provided a soil test shows that fertilizer is, in fact, needed. It's important not to deprive the plant of nitrogen or other nutrients following planting.

You can apply fertilizer by spreading it on the soil surface, or by adding it to the planting hole. Much has been said and written to warn gardeners that fertilizer in the planting hole causes root damage, a bugaboo probably based on experiments in the 1920s and 30s when the principal form of nitrogen fertilizer was sodium nitrate. Fertilizers are salts. Those with a high salt index—the measure of saltiness—may absorb water that roots need when the soil is dry. Leaves die, and the damage is misleadingly called fertilizer burn. Today, though, there are forms of nitrogen fertilizer that can be added to the planting hole safely. For example, urea, one of the most widely available forms of nitrogen fertilizer, has a salt index of 1.6 per unit of nitrogen, far less than the salt index of sodium nitrate—6.1.

Test the soil before you plant, and apply no more fertilizer than the soil test calls for. (Any fertilizer applied at excessive rates can cause problems.) If fertilizer is needed, choose one with a low salt index. To supply nitrogen, look for a formulation that includes ureaformaldehyde, IBDU (isobutylene diurea) or ammoniated phosphate. If your soil has a phosphorus deficiency, incorporate superphosphate (with an analysis of 0-20-0) or triple superphosphate (0-46-0) into the soil as the test results suggest. (It is important to note that phosphorus does not move through the soil. It must be mixed into the root zone in order to be readily available

How to Plant a Shrub or Tree

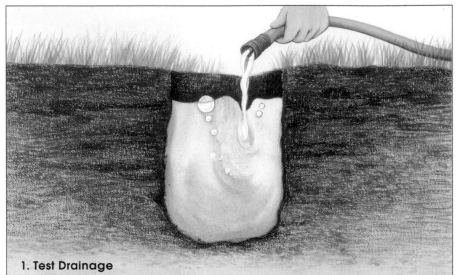

1. Test Drainage
Dig a hole 8 in. wide and 12 in. deep at the planting site. Fill the hole with water several times during the day, then one last time in the evening. If there is still water in the hole 24 hours later, consider planting in a better-drained location.

2. Dig a Wide Planting Hole
Dig a hole at least twice as wide as the root system, and the same depth. If your plant is balled and burlapped, remove the strings and pull the burlap away from the root ball before backfilling.

to plants.) The salt index of superphosphate and triple superphosphate is near zero. If you have to add potassium, be aware that potassium chloride (muriate of potash), the most common potassium source, has a *very high* salt index. Use it with care.

In general, fertilizers derived from organic sources pose little risk of salt damage because they release nutrients very slowly. Slow-release or controlled-release chemical fertilizers offer the same advantage; even if they contain nutrients in forms that have high salt indices, they become available to plants so slowly that they are

unlikely to cause any harm. Organic and other slow-release fertilizers cost more initially, but they don't need to be applied as frequently.

In good soils, fertilizing at planting time has little impact on the first flush of top growth following planting. That growth is influenced mostly by growing conditions the previous summer and fall, when buds were formed. However, remember that fertilizing at, or shortly after, planting encourages additional growth that year and promotes bud development the first fall following planting. These buds will produce the spring flush of growth one

Illustrations: Pat Schories

3. Fertilize as Needed
Apply fertilizer in amounts suggested by a soil test directly to the planting hole or to the soil after planting.

4. Mulch and Water
Mulch a wide area around the plant to a depth of 2 in. to 4 in., but no more than 2 in. around the trunk. Water thoroughly after planting, then supplement rainfall throughout the first growing season.

year after planting, and it's that growth that reflects how "happy" the plant is in the new site.

Lay on the mulch
Young shrubs and trees do better when competition is kept in check, and mulch is the best way to supply the relief they need. Mulch suppresses weeds, conserves moisture, checks erosion, prevents soil compaction in heavy rains and moderates soil temperature. Pine bark, aged woodchips, pine straw, chopped leaves—most organic materials, in fact—work well as mulch.

Apply mulch to a sizable area around a newly-planted tree or shrub— the roots will eventually extend far from the trunk. The right depth for mulch is 2 in. to 4 in., depending on the type of soil it covers. Less mulch is required for heavy soils, more for light soils. In either case, mulch that is too deep can cause problems. It can prevent the soil from drying out, depriving plant roots of necessary oxygen. Extremely deep mulch also may encourage rodents which can damage plant stems. Do not place mulch more than 2 in. deep next to the stem of a tree or shrub. An excessively deep, fine-textured mulch around the stem may kill the bark near the soil line, resulting in the eventual death of the entire plant.

Keep in mind that organic mulches may temporarily tie up a substantial portion of soil nitrogen, which is used by the microorganisms that break down the mulch. In time, the nitrogen bound by the microorganisms will be released, but in the short run, additional nitrogen may be required to support vigorous growth of new plantings. To prevent problems, broadcast a bit of nitrogen fertilizer on the soil before you mulch.

Water diligently
All plants need soil with adequate moisture, especially while their root systems are growing rapidly. Water is the necessary ingredient for plant growth that is most often in short supply. If rain falls short, make up the deficit by watering deeply every five to seven days, taking care not to suffocate roots by overwatering. In my research, supplemental watering throughout the first growing season made an enormous difference in the growth of transplanted shrubs and trees.

I recommend drip irrigation systems whenever possible. They conserve moisture, while minimizing the liability of overwatering. Since you don't wet the foliage, you don't encourage leaf diseases. The key to using drip irrigation is to water thoroughly, then allow the soil to dry moderately before watering again. Placing mulch over the drip system helps slow evaporation of moisture from the soil.

Start with a healthy plant
I have one last suggestion to offer about planting shrubs and trees: select only thrifty plants, those grown properly at the nursery and handled with care before sale. Thrifty plants are those with good, deep leaf color and plump stems and buds. The key to successful transplant establishment is the energy *inside* the plant. This is more important than what is done outside the plant. All the care in the world cannot make a sickly plant thrive.

Once you have chosen a healthy specimen, it is up to you to provide the conditions that will enable the plant to adapt to its new site and prosper there. Give it a wide hole, the necessary fertilizer, mulch and plenty of water, and it will reward you with vigorous growth. □

Carl Whitcomb, PhD, is a consultant to the nursery industry and author of several books, including Establishment and Maintenance of Landscape Plants *($31.00 ppd., Lacebark, Inc., P.O. Box 2383, Stillwater, OK 74076). He lives in Stillwater, Oklahoma.*

A Better Start for Container-Grown Trees

Copper paint prevents pot-bound roots

by Daniel K. Struve

When a gardener buys a young shrub or tree, the root system largely decides what happens next. If the roots are intact, they soon resume growth, and the plant establishes itself quickly. Unfortunately, after transplanting, few root systems are intact. Field-grown plants lose a lot of roots when they're dug, and plants grown in containers often become pot-bound and must be root-pruned at transplanting.

Here at Ohio State University, where I'm an associate professor of horticulture, we've found that coating containers with a copper-bearing paint produces root systems that need no pruning. Since 1985, I and two graduate students, Mike Arnold and David Chinery, have trialed a number of species of deciduous trees, among them green ash, red oak, Shumard's oak and several red maple cultivars, as well as many shrubs, including viburnums, witch hazels, rhododendrons and azaleas. All respond well to our painted containers. We think nursery-

Author Struve has found that containers coated on the inside with a homemade copper-bearing paint prevent seedling shrubs and trees from developing circling roots. In the photos above, two yellow buckeyes (*Aesculus octandra*)—the one on the left grown in a painted container and the other in a standard container—have been unpotted after one season (top) and the soil washed away (above). Root tips stop elongating when they approach the copper paint, prompting the inhibited roots to branch.

men will try the method, and gardeners should, too.

Root problems

Whether field-grown plants are dug by machine or by hand, they lose roots. Bare-root plants generally retain only their largest roots, and balled-and-burlapped plants fare little better. Both harvest methods leave a high percentage of root tips in the field. Root tips are the part of the root system capable of rapid elongation, and they contribute most to initial plant establishment. With good care—mainly diligent watering—field-grown trees will survive transplanting reasonably

well and in two or three years will be growing vigorously. Without adequate moisture, however, the root system will struggle and not make much growth. Under these conditions, the plant may die outright, or make very little growth for two or three years.

Growing shrubs and trees in containers seems to promise intact root systems, but in practice the roots often need pruning at transplanting. A container-grown plant tends to become pot-bound, developing a mat of roots at the bottom of the pot and prominent circling roots (photos at left). To ensure long-term survival and growth, it's standard practice when transplanting to slice the sides of the root ball and cut off the mat on the bottom, though root pruning largely undoes the advantages of container growing. Root-pruned plants need good care and take several years to resume vigorous growth. Without pruning, the root ball struggles to develop, and can choke itself. Only a few roots escape to grow into the soil, and the circling roots can girdle each other and the stem of the plant. An afflicted plant grows poorly and lacks the anchoring and the drought tolerance of plants with unconstricted roots.

Researchers have tried to mitigate the drawbacks of containers by altering their shapes. They've embossed vertical ridges and pyramidal staircases in containers to halt and deflect roots and prevent circling, with some success. They've tried open-bottomed containers, and containers with perforated sides, for similar reasons and with similar success. One of the more promising recent innovations is the root-control container, commonly called a grow bag, which has a fibrous wall that traps root tips and by constriction prevents them from elongating.

Painted containers

We grow young shrubs and trees in standard, round, plastic nursery containers that we've painted on the inside with a homemade mix of latex paint and cupric carbonate, a copper compound. When root tips approach the sides and bottom of the painted containers, they stop elongating, inhibited (but not harmed) by the copper. New lateral roots then develop from the old roots, the cycle repeats, and in one season the seedling develops a much-branched mass of roots (which the nursery trade often refers to as a "fibrous" root system), with many root tips throughout the root ball and around the periphery. Our plants need little or no root pruning. While no one understands how copper inhibits root elongation, we know that the effect is transient. We've observed roots through a glass window and found that they resume elongating at their former rate within a week of transplanting. The plants establish themselves more quickly and produce more growth for a year or two than do plants we grow by other methods.

In our trials, plants from painted containers consistently outperform plants grown by conventional methods in the year or two after transplanting. The differences are most dramatic when trees grown in painted containers and bare-root field-grown trees — especially whips — are transplanted into the field. In the nursery business, whips are slender

Struve adds powdered cupric carbonate, a copper-bearing compound, to exterior latex paint (above) to produce a mix that, when applied to containers, controls root development. With a sponge, he spreads the mixture evenly inside a standard 1-gal. pot (below). Cupric carbonate is a caustic irritant. Gloves and careful handling are needed to avoid skin contact and inhalation of the powder.

young trees between 5 ft. and 8 ft. tall, generally branchless or with a few short slender branches near the top of the trunk. Though they're sold as one-year-old plants, it's often taken the nursery three years or longer to grow them.

In the fall of 1986, we transplanted seven-month-old red oak whips grown in copper-painted containers and three-year-old bare-root field-grown whips to a test plot. We also transplanted three-year-old bare-root field-grown whips to the plot in the spring of 1987. The bare-root whips came from a nursery on the West Coast, as do many whips sold by retail nurseries in our area. In spite of their different ages, the trees were of similar size, 5 ft. to 6 ft. tall. In all, we transplanted 120 container-grown and 30 bare-root whips. During the 1987 growing season, which had 6 in. to 9 in. less rainfall than normal, the trees received no irrigation. The container-grown whips produced 18 in. of growth, and the bare-root whips made 6 in. of growth. Eleven of the 30 bare-root whips died. All the container-grown whips survived.

In another trial, we looked at transplant shock. We transplanted year-old trees grown in painted containers and year-old trees grown in ordinary containers, setting them out in July to subject them to high temperatures. As before, we did not irrigate them. Then we counted the days until leaf burn, a convenient measure of transplant shock. All the trees stopped growing after transplanting, but the trees from ordinary containers had brown leaf edges in 29 days, while the trees from painted containers took 45 days to show distress.

Homegrown plants

You can readily adapt our methods to your conditions. You need seeds or small seedlings, a porous potting mix, fertilizer, 1-gal. and 3-gal. containers, and a sunny location. You also have to be prepared to water and fertilize the plants and control pests throughout the growing season. If you plan a vacation, you'll need an automatic irrigation system or a trustworthy friend.

Painting the containers is straightforward. We buy cupric carbonate in powder form and combine 3.4 oz. (about 6 tbsp.) of the powder with 1 qt. of exterior latex paint, which makes enough mix for 125 one-gal. pots. We've also found that copper sulfate in similar quantities had much the same effect on forsythia plants as cupric carbonate did, and we think it will work for other woody plants and trees. (To buy cupric carbonate, contact Norinberg Scientific, 6310 Southwest Virginia, Portland, OR 97201; 503-246-8297. The minimum order is $20. Copper sulfate is used as an algicide in ponds and is available at many garden centers.)

Cupric carbonate is classified as a caustic irritant. We wear rubber gloves and are careful to keep it off our skin, and we pour the powder and mix the paint slowly to avoid raising dust. Though copper isn't nearly as toxic as some metals, such as mercury, it should be handled with care.

The cupric carbonate and latex paint make a thick slurry, which we swab on the inside of the containers with an ordinary household sponge. We've painted fiber and plastic containers, and both types have provided good root control for one season. The paint lasts three seasons on plastic containers before it starts to flake off, but we're not sure that it controls root growth adequately after the first season. We prefer to repaint the containers each year.

We start seeds in flats. When the primary root first emerges, we transplant each seed to a 1-gal. container filled with a potting mix of 3 parts composted shredded pine bark, 1 part sand and 1 part peat. You can use any porous potting mix, and the same container and mix would be suitable for tiny seedlings, too. When the germinating seed or young seedling goes into the container, we spread 1 tbsp. of 18-6-12 Osmocote, a slow-release fertilizer, atop the potting mix. From then on we fertilize weekly with a solution of ½ tbsp. 20-20-20 fertilizer to 1 gal. of water.

We give our trees an early start in controlled conditions in a greenhouse, but you don't need a greenhouse to start trees—just sow germinating seeds or transplant young seedlings after the last frost. Your trees may be smaller at the end of the season than ours are, but they will still be good-size. Where we produce 5-ft.-tall trees, you might grow 3½-ft.-tall trees. If you enjoy a seven- or eight-month growing season, you can probably grow seedlings the size we do without a greenhouse.

After the last frost, we take our seedlings out of the greenhouse, give them two weeks to acclimate under shade cloth, and then repot them in cupric-

When root tips approach the sides or bottom of a painted container, they cease elongating, inhibited by the copper in the paint. The root then branches, and the cycle repeats. This produces a fibrous root system, like the one shown above. The inhibition is transient. After transplanting, all the root tips of the root system will resume elongating within days.

carbonate-treated 3-gal. containers. For seedlings started after the last frost, you'll probably have to repot sometime during the season. Starting in midsummer, try gently unpotting each tree from time to time. If the potting mix crumbles, stop; if it comes free in a mass, it's time to repot the tree

in a 3-gal. container. You won't see a mat of roots at the bottom of the root ball, or many white root tips on the sides. The copper treatment inhibits root elongation before the root tips contact the container. If your growing season is short, and the end is in sight, you should probably not repot. If you do,

the seedling may continue growing late in the fall and fail to harden properly for the winter.

After moving a seedling to a 3-gal. container, we spread 2 tbsp. of 18-6-12 Osmocote on the potting mix. Then we resume fertilizing with the same dilution of 20-20-20 water-soluble fertilizer we use for 1-gal. containers. To encourage a straight trunk, we loosely tie the rapidly elongating terminal shoot to a bamboo stake at 9-in. intervals. About mid-September, six weeks or so before the first frost, we reduce watering. The seedling's shoots soon stop elongating and begin to enter dormancy. The trunk continues to thicken, however, and the roots continue to grow for some time longer.

Once your seedlings go dormant, you have two options. The easiest is to transplant them. The soil temperature is still warm enough for root growth, and the root tips will continue elongating until the soil grows cold, provided they have enough moisture. If you want to transplant in spring, you can overwinter the plants in their containers. Deciduous plants will overwinter in the dark, but for conifers some light is needed to prevent yellowing of the foliage. Keep the plants at near-freezing temperatures, but do not permit the roots to endure temperatures below 28°F or they'll suffer injury. If you can't provide minimum heat, you can leave the plants outdoors, lay them on their sides, and insulate them with a sandwich of straw and plastic. You'll have to fence the plants or spread poison bait to keep them safe from rodents. Uncover the plants in spring when the minimum temperature remains above 28°F. Ideally, you should transplant them as early as you can work the soil, but we have held plants in containers for months with good results. Whether you transplant in fall or spring, water the plants regularly. Even an ideal root system needs water to grow. □

Daniel Struve is an associate professor of horticulture at Ohio State University in Columbus, Ohio.

Unshearing Shrubs
Selective pruning restores natural open form

by Cass Turnbull

Andrea opened my eyes. Years ago when I worked for a city park department, my crew took pride in keeping junipers, dogwoods, spireas and azaleas neatly sheared, and the public complimented us for our work. Then the park department hired Andrea, a horticulturist, to teach us about plants. Walking through the park, observing our careful shearing,

Removing dead and crowded branches from the interior opens the canopy of once-sheared shrubs and lets in light and air. Above, author Turnbull works inside a strawberry tree.

she said, "It's a crime against nature." I was surprised and confused at first, but eventually I understood that selective pruning is more appropriate than shearing for most shrubs. It respects their natural form and is less threatening to their health. As a bonus, it's easier on the gardener.

I have to admit that shearing has its place when formality and contrast are important, as in hedges or topiary, and

Repeated shearing develops a dense canopy of leaves and twigs, as shown here. The shrub's natural shape gives way to a geometric silhouette, with all the branches hidden.

What shearing does

With each shearing, indicated by the dotted lines in the drawings, more branches are cut back, then more branches grow out. The shrub develops a thin, dense, twiggy canopy (leaves have been omitted here for clarity). New branches, shown in green, often grow vigorously, so the shrub needs frequent shearing to look neat. Shaded by the canopy, the interior of the shrub stops growing: leaves and twigs die, and fallen leaves catch in the branches, inviting pests and diseases.

First shearing

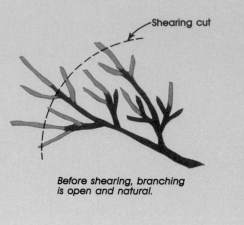

Shearing cut

Before shearing, branching is open and natural.

---

knot, rose and Japanese-style gardens. But I don't believe that sheared shrubbery makes a conventional yard look tidy and interesting. To me, it's an eyesore. I confess that I sometimes resort to mockery and call sheared shrubs "poodleballs," "hockey pucks" and "green meatballs."

In my landscaping business, I help gardeners unshear their shrubs. When a client calls, I often find a close-cropped bun of leaves. In a few years, I transform it into an open framework of branches with

a graceful, natural-looking canopy. The process takes judicious pruning in small doses. I'll show you how I do it, but first I'll talk about the drawbacks of shearing.

What's wrong with shearing?

For one thing, few shrubs are well suited to shearing. The ideal candidate is tough enough to take repeated shearing, and regrows from old branches if you must prune away its leafy shell. The best plants also have small evergreen leaves, so they

look neat and attractive all year. Among conifers, only fine-needled yews, junipers, hemlocks and arborvitae look tidy when sheared, and only the yew reliably produces new growth when cut back to branches three years old or older. There are relatively few good broadleaf evergreens for shearing, among them boxwood, Japanese holly, privet, pyracantha, evergreen azalea and box honeysuckle. All are rugged and small-leaved.

Shearing wastes the beauty of many

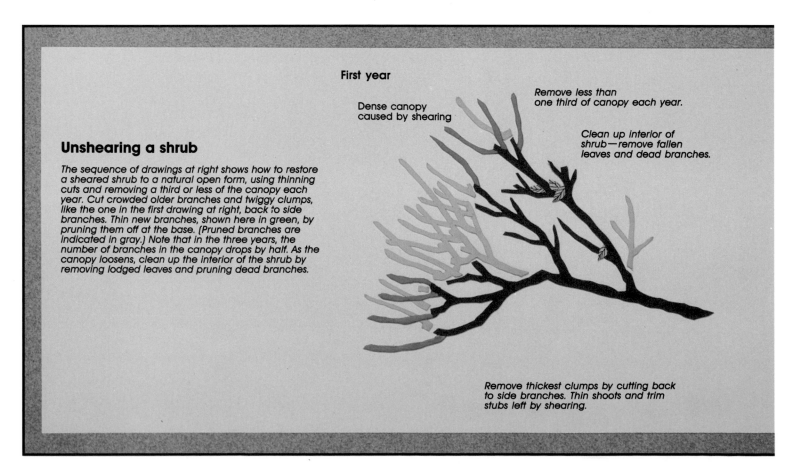

Unshearing a shrub

The sequence of drawings at right shows how to restore a sheared shrub to a natural open form, using thinning cuts and removing a third or less of the canopy each year. Cut crowded older branches and twiggy clumps, like the one in the first drawing at right, back to side branches. Thin new branches, shown here in green, by pruning them off at the base. (Pruned branches are indicated in gray.) Note that in the three years, the number of branches in the canopy drops by half. As the canopy loosens, clean up the interior of the shrub by removing lodged leaves and pruning dead branches.

First year

Dense canopy caused by shearing

Remove less than one third of canopy each year.

Clean up interior of shrub—remove fallen leaves and dead branches.

Remove thickest clumps by cutting back to side branches. Thin shoots and trim stubs left by shearing.

Illustrations: Laura B. Goodwin

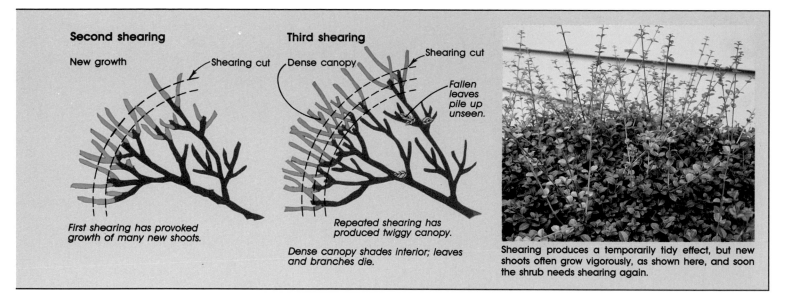

Second shearing

New growth — Shearing cut

First shearing has provoked growth of many new shoots.

Third shearing

Dense canopy — Shearing cut

Fallen leaves pile up unseen.

Repeated shearing has produced twiggy canopy.

Dense canopy shades interior; leaves and branches die.

Shearing produces a temporarily tidy effect, but new shoots often grow vigorously, as shown here, and soon the shrub needs shearing again.

shrubs. I know gardeners who have never seen their shrubs bloom because they shear the plants when flower buds are forming. They could shear after flowering, but they'd have to tolerate shrubs that looked a little long-haired. I'd rather have a graceful shrub with flowers than a tidy one without. In addition, shearing hides or destroys the beautiful bark and branching of plants such as the camellia, strawberry tree, azalea, Japanese maple and eastern dogwood (believe it or not,

people in Seattle lollipop them).

Branches and flowers aside, shearing also limits the richness of a landscape. Where there could be striking contrasts of texture and form, shearing imposes uniformity. The fine-leaved boxwood and the bold-leaved viburnum lose their character when sheared. A weeping Alaska cedar and an angular 'Pfitzer' juniper contrast nicely when you prune naturally, but not when you shear.

Worst of all, shearing locks you into a

high-maintenance routine. To explain why, I have to talk about the two basic pruning cuts, "thinning" and "heading." When you prune a branch back to its parent branch or to the ground, you've made a thinning cut. When you shorten a branch by pruning anywhere between its tip and its base, you've made a heading cut. Since heading almost always encourages shoots to grow rapidly from the remaining buds and twigs on the branch, and often prompts dormant buds to pro-

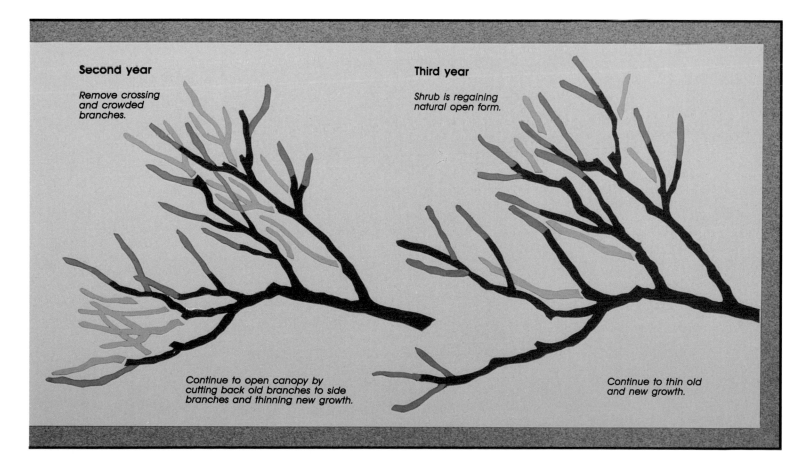

Second year

Remove crossing and crowded branches.

Continue to open canopy by cutting back old branches to side branches and thinning new growth.

Third year

Shrub is regaining natural open form.

Continue to thin old and new growth.

duce shoots as well, you soon get a crowd of new shoots around a heading cut. Shearing is basically wholesale heading. So year by year, a sheared shrub grows a little larger and a lot twiggier (see the drawings at the top of pp. 44-45). New shoots grow rapidly after shearing, as the shrub struggles to replace lost leaves. Within weeks or months, you have to shear again.

Furthermore, shearing threatens a shrub's health. As a shrub hastens to replace lost leaves, it expends energy reserves to produce rapidly growing new shoots, which are susceptible to drought, cold, pests and diseases. Many shrubs lack the stamina to rebound—barberry and spirea, for example, develop dead spots with repeated shearing. Vigorous shrubs tolerate shearing, but they still suffer stress. One last drawback of shearing: The dense canopy shades a shrub's interior. For lack of sunlight, a leafless zone develops, and eventually twigs die. Meanwhile, fallen leaves catch in the branches, making "bird's nests" that invite pests and diseases.

Unshearing

How do you restore sheared shrubs to their natural shape? Thin selectively, removing some of the twiggy canopy each year, and let time do the rest. You can unshear at any time of the year. I divide shrubs into two basic categories and prune them differently. The plants in the first group have a few main stems, and most branches rebranch repeatedly; deciduous azaleas are a good example. I prune this type of shrub with restraint, cutting unwanted branches back to side branches or buds. Members of the second group, which I call cane-growers, make a cluster of stems that branch very little, if at all; forsythias are representative of this category. The plants in this group are tough and renew themselves readily from the base. I restore them by cutting a few stems off at the base and thinning a little each year.

Have the right gear when you start. Use a good pair of bypass shears, the kind with curved blades that slide past each other. They cut cleanly and leave no stub when you cut a branch at the base. Have a pruning saw on hand, too. I like the small saws with folding blades. They fit in a pocket, and work in tight quarters. I usually wear leather gloves— sheared shrubs are scratchy.

Cane-growers are easier to unshear than much-branched shrubs are. Each year, you remove a few of the biggest, oldest stems, cutting them as close as possible to the crown of the plant or to the ground. If hand shears won't work, use the pruning saw. Also look in the canopy for the most snarled, twiggiest branches and cut them back to a side branch or bud, preferably one that faces outward so new growth will leave the interior open.

Remove no more than one third of the canopy each year. If you take too much, the plant tries to recoup by suckering profusely from the ground and the remaining branches. The new shoots grow rapidly and make a bigger pruning job the next year.

For some very old shrubs, radical renovation may be in order. It's a drastic treatment—rather than thin gradually for several years, you cut the shrub clear to the ground all at once. Only tough deciduous cane-growing shrubs, such as forsythia, philadelphus, deutzia, kolkwitzia

Turnbull has been unshearing this zable laurel for three years. She has softened its silhouette and developed an attractive pattern of branches.

and potentilla, tolerate radical renovation; they resprout readily from the crown and roots. Keep in mind that a cut-back shrub needs three years or more to look good again and to flower. You can also expect the shrub to regain its former size. The big root system of an old plant has lots of energy for regrowth.

With much-branched shrubs, the hardest part is getting started. You can take three approaches: snip a lot of twigs, thin small branches, or cut out the worst twiggy clumps. I recommend that you combine all three practices, but concentrate on the last. First, choose a portion of the canopy about a foot square. Then run a hand over it, feeling for the thickest clump of twigs. Push the clump aside to see how it branches, and prune it off with a thinning cut, as the drawings at the bottom of pp. 44-45 illustrate. Proceed around the canopy, section by section. Thin equally for the most part, but a bit more heavily around the base of the shrub than on the top to soften the look of a box, ball or bun. Finish the whole canopy, then go

back over it a square foot at a time, cutting out a few crossing twigs and small branches, and call it a day.

When you step back for a look, be prepared to see very little change. Long-sheared shrubs need time to resume natural shapes. Where you remove clumps the first year, nearby branches spring into the gap. Resist the urge to keep pruning. On many shrubs, heavy thinning invites trouble. If you remove more than an eighth to a third of the canopy at a time, you stress the shrub and provoke it into producing rapidly growing shoots.

The next year, prune again. Take out the worst clumps and branches as you did the first year, and look for new growth that needs thinning. With light reaching the shrub's interior for the first time in years, long-dormant buds come to life. Shoots develop and reach out to the canopy. Remove some entirely, head others back, or head back the parent branch (the drawings show all three choices).

The sheared silhouette eventually breaks up. By the second year, the base of the shrub opens a little, and the canopy starts to exhibit rolling contours. By the third year, the original layer of twigs is almost gone, and the shrub is evolving a natural pattern of branches.

The interior of a sheared shrub needs work, too. With big shrubs, I like to step inside the canopy and work up and out from the bottom. Whether you work from the inside or the outside, clean out leaves hung up in the forks of branches, and prune off all dead branches. Remove any branch that starts on one side, heads through the center and grows out the other side. Cut out the worst of the branches that cross or rub other branches. As you thin wayward branches, step back frequently to check your progress. It's easy to cut too much. Heed the old saying: "Wander, ponder, and prune."

A final plea

I hope I've persuaded you to prune rather than shear. But if you're not swayed yet, consider two last points. Sheared shrubs get bigger every year and eventually outgrow their site. If the shrub will regrow from old branches, you can cut it back drastically. You'll soon face the challenge of pruning a forest of vigorous new shoots, however. By contrast, if you prune shrubs to natural shapes, you can control their growth with thinning cuts. Finally, pruning is a lot less work than shearing. An hour a year will take care of most shrubs. Wouldn't you like to use the time you spend shearing to enjoy healthy, naturally shaped shrubs instead? □

Cass Turnbull is the founder of Plant Amnesty, a nonprofit group that promotes good pruning. She is a professional gardener in Seattle, Washington.

Standardizing

Training plants to a formal shape

by Tovah Martin

Like those lollipop-shaped trees that children draw in kindergarten, standards are plants trained to grow a dense ball of foliage atop a straight, slender stem. It takes a skilled gardener to coax plants into such a neat, formal shape—they wouldn't naturally grow that way. Standardizing is a horticultural challenge, and even more, it's an artistic endeavor.

As with other forms of topiary, training standards is an ancient art, first mastered by the Romans. Today, few growers have the experience and patience for it. For those growers willing to tackle the challenge, though, the rewards are well worth the effort. A well-grown, mature standard is a masterpiece that can fetch $500 or serve as a family heirloom. But the monetary value of the plant is only part of the picture. More important is the sense of accomplishment you get from spending years successfully sculpting nature.

Traditionally, standards travel in pairs. About a dozen years ago, at the greenhouses where I work, we made our first standard—a 4-ft.-tall small-leaved myrtle topped with a 2½-ft. crown. It was three years in the making, and we decided to synchronize its unveiling with the arrival of an interested customer. She was duly impressed, and said she'd take them. Them? It had no twin. That orphan standard is still in our care.

Typically, paired standards are stationed on either side of an entry, like those ferocious marble lions that guard government buildings. They create an atmosphere of formality even before you enter the gate. In that capacity, standards are used in gardens and greenhouses, to flank French windows, or as front-door sentinels. Especially if you have trained it yourself, you might be delighted to display a single standard as the focal point of a garden, greenhouse or bay window. But if you want to end up with a perfect pair, play it safe and start with a trio. Later, you can choose the two most closely matched.

We grow all our standards in containers, but it's possible to train plants growing out in a garden bed. Many plants can be made into standards. Basically, any bushy plant with compact, upright growth can be shaped into a tree-like form. First, you have to train a single shoot to grow into a straight, sturdy, upright trunk. Then you must prune and reprune the branches at the top of the trunk until they grow to form a dense, leafy crown. Careful clipping develops the crown into a ball, cone or other shape.

I prefer standards made from woody plants with small, close-set, evergreen leaves. These plants will produce a tight, gapless crown. Plants with softer stems and larger leaves can be shaped into looser, less formal standards. Hibiscus, roses, pelargoniums (geraniums), coleus and even poinsettias are often chosen for the purpose, although horticulturists usually apply a growth retardant to larger-growing specimens to keep the crowns compact. When flowering plants are made into standards, you can enjoy the bonus of blossoms on the finished orb. The blossoms will be more abundant than on untrained plants, but each will be smaller.

One of the best-suited plants for training into standard form is the small-leaved myrtle (*Myrtus communis* 'Microphylla'). This is the Biblical myrtle, not to be confused with creeping myrtle or crape myrtle. Cultivated in gardens since Biblical days, myrtle is an evergreen shrub native to the Mediterranean region. In nature, it grows as a dense, broad bush up to 10 ft. tall. The small-leaved form has shiny dark leaves about ½ in. long that release a pleasant fragrance when cut or bruised. In the spring, myrtle bears hundreds of small, fluffy white flowers.

Myrtle is well qualified for standardizing because it's easy to train a growing shoot into a strong stem. Its close-set leaves fully hide the mass of tiny twigs in the crown. Myrtle is a trouble-free plant, not prone to disease or attack by insects. In fact, the only drawback is its slow growth. Myrtle will not become an "instant" standard. It takes more than two years to train a myrtle, but the end result

is far superior to the loose, airy standards fashioned in a single season from fast-growing plants such as coleus.

As you train a myrtle standard, you'll need to provide for its basic requirements: light and warmth, fertile soil, and water. If you live in an area with a Mediterranean climate, you can grow myrtle outdoors year round. In Connecticut, we carry our myrtle standards out of the greenhouses after the last frost in spring, and bring them back in before the first frost in fall. They thrive outdoors in the bright light and long days of summer. You should always acclimate plants slowly to the outdoor environment, though, as even plants can sunburn. Set them in the shade for a week before putting them in full sun. Standards can easily tip over and break, so be sure that they are protected from hard rains, wind, hail or other drastic weather. We often bury the pots to their rim in the ground. This steadies them, and also keeps the clay pots from drying out rapidly, which means we don't have to water quite as often.

Except for the summer months, we grow myrtle inside. A greenhouse is the ideal indoor environment, since it provides uniform bright light. Second best is a bright sunroom or sunporch. A sunny, south-facing window will do if you rotate the plant often to expose all sides to the light. If you forget to turn the plant, the stem frequently will begin to lean precariously toward one side, and once it has grown lopsided it's hard to straighten it up again.

The challenge in growing myrtle as a houseplant in the winter is providing a location that is sufficiently cool and bright. With temperatures between 50° and 65°F and plenty of light, myrtle will continue to grow throughout the winter. It does no harm if the thermometer dips to 40°F, but the foliage will start to acquire a reddish tinge and the plant will not make active growth. If room temperatures stay above 65°F and the plant receives only weak sunlight for a few hours a day, myrtle will grow soft, elongated stems.

Throughout the year, water myrtle when the soil surface is dry to the touch. During active growth, feed about every three weeks with 20-20-20 or another balanced fertilizer, diluted according to the directions on the label. Cut back on fertilizing during the winter months (once every six to eight weeks is enough); the plant uses less fertilizer when days are short and light is scant.

A myrtle needs repotting several times as it grows into a standard. You can tell when it's ready to be repotted by checking the roots. Tip the plant upside down, fit your first and second fingers around the stem, and tap the pot against the edge of a bench or a table so that the root ball falls free from the pot. If the roots form a white mass that fills the soil, it's time to repot. If there's still plenty of soil between and around the visible roots, slide the same pot back in place. (This checking doesn't hurt the plant, and it's the best way to monitor root growth.)

Over the years, you'll transplant the myrtle from its original 2½-in. pot to a 4-in. pot, then into a 6-in. pot, and so on until you reach a 12-in. pot. You might be tempted to take shortcuts by jumping more than one pot size at a time, but most growers recommend a gradual shifting. A small plant won't grow any faster because you've put it in a large pot, and you risk overwatering it. Wait until the roots fill the soil in each size pot, and then transplant the myrtle into a bigger pot.

To repot, put a little soil in the bottom of the new pot before setting the myrtle in place; don't bury the stem any deeper than it was before. Add extra soil to fill the gap between the root ball and the new pot. Try not to disturb the root ball, but use your finger or a pencil to tamp down the soil and wedge it in around the edges. Water well to settle the soil.

We prefer clay pots. Clay drains well, and it provides ballast when a standard reaches its top-heavy stage. We often use the shallow, broad-based, "azalea" type pots because the standards are less liable

to tip over in a breeze. We also use a heavy, humusy soil rather than a light, peat-based mix. Our recipe combines compost, soil, peat moss, sand and vermiculite in a 1:3:4:4:1 ratio, with small amounts of lime and fertilizer added to each batch.

Although a mature standard needs continual pruning, it does not require further repotting. Once a year, lift it out of the pot to check the root system. Prune off any dead or brown roots, top-dress that pot with fresh soil to replace any that has eroded away, and continue to fertilize the plant. A myrtle standard will grow perfectly well in a 12-in. container indefinitely.

The fun and challenge of making a standard is in the training process. I suggest that you start by training a myrtle into a lollipop shape. Here I'll describe creating a 2½-ft.-tall standard with a 10-in.-dia. crown. Of course, you can train standards to any height and shape you desire, but do give some thought to the balance involved. You don't want to create a bird's nest atop a telephone pole or an elephant atop a toothpick. Also bear in mind the setting in which you plan to exhibit your standards—their ultimate height and shape should be influenced by where you will be displaying them. (Don't forget to allow for the height of the pots.) In my opinion, a 2½-ft. standard is ideal for viewing head-on, but you can add or subtract a few inches for taller or shorter standards.

Myrtles begin new growth in March, and this is a fine time to start training one as a standard. Start with a young plant in a 2½-in. pot (see Sources, facing page). A good candidate has a straight, upright stem that is not branched or pinched at the top. (If you're mail-ordering a plant, specify that you want a single-stemmed plant for training into a standard.) That stem, called the leader, will become the

monopod on which the crown is balanced. It cannot be pinched or pruned until the standard has attained its full height.

As soon as the plant is about 6 in. tall, remove the lower 2 in. of leaves. Clip the remaining branches close to the stem so that the myrtle is only 1 in. to 2 in. wide. Myrtle grows in height and width 1 in. to 3 in. a month or faster, depending on how much warmth and light it receives. During this phase of the training process, the standard should look like a bottlebrush, with a 4-in.-long section of bristle-like branches atop a thin, handle-like stem. Check the plant every few weeks, and keep the bottom of the stem clear of branches. If the branches are soft, you can remove them by running your fingers down the stem. If they are larger than toothpicks and getting woody, use shears to prune them off close to the stem, being very careful not to damage or sever the leader.

When the leader has reached a foot in height, it needs the support of a stake. A piece of pencil-thin bamboo about 18 in. tall makes a good support. Push it down an inch or more into the soil right near the stem, making sure that the stake is absolutely straight up and down. Then bind the stem closely to the stake with twist-ties, tying one about 4 in. from the base, and another about 4 in. above the first. If the stem has any crooks or bends, add a tie at the point of the problem spot to straighten out the defect.

Even during the winter, myrtle may grow an inch taller each month. Keep denuding the bottom of the stem while allowing the leader to grow, always retaining the top 4 in. of foliage, trimmed to a brushy column. When the base of the foliage is 20 in. high, it has reached the beginning point for the orb. You might want to mark this milestone by tying a piece of ribbon at that height. As the plant grows on, continue to denude the stem below the 20-in.

Choose a myrtle with a single upright stem (on the left). A bushy plant (on the right) doesn't have a leader and can't be trained into a standard.

Tie the leader to a bamboo stake and trim the side branches into a column. As the plant grows, remove the bottom foliage, retaining the top 4 in.

When the myrtle has outgrown its first stake, insert a longer one, securing the stem every 4 in. with twist-ties.

mark, but now let the foliage grow up with the leader, keeping it clipped to a narrow column. Continue to tie the stem every 4 in. as the plant grows—this is particularly important in the winter, when new growth tends to be weaker than that produced during sunnier seasons.

The stake must support the entire height of the stem to keep the stem from wobbling, and to ensure that its growth will be as straight as an arrow. When the leader has outgrown its original stake, replace it with a longer, stronger one. We usually insert a new stake at the same time as we repot a standard.

Soon after the standard is a year old, it should reach its full 30-in. height. When it does, you can stop worrying about the leader. In fact, you should pinch or clip the leader to stop any further upward growth. It is now time to start work on the crown.

There are two ways to go about growing a myrtle's crown: the fast way, and the slow way. Having tolerated an ugly duckling for a year, many people become impatient for a finished product, so they allow the top branches to grow out unchecked and form a loose crown. The result is not bad-looking, but it is not a masterpiece. A much handsomer, formal specimen comes from continual pruning, encouraging the myrtle to branch out and branch out again until it has formed a thick, gapless ball.

Each shearing has the effect of multiplying the number of branches. This response is controlled by the plant hormone auxin, which is produced in the growing tip, or apex, of every branch on the myrtle. As it passes downward through a stem, auxin inhibits the development of lateral buds—a phenomenon called apical dominance. When you remove the tip and stop the flow of auxin, these buds are free to grow into new shoots. Repeated pruning of the tips eventually produces a

thick mass of intertwining branches. Myrtle responds especially well to this treatment.

The myrtle's crown will grow out about 2 in. a month, or faster, particularly if the plant is growing outdoors in the summer. As often as the shoots grow out 2 in., clip them back 1 in. It's two steps forward, one step back. You'll probably need to trim more off the top than off the sides, to keep the height the same while increasing the width of the ball. Envision that you are gradually transforming the thin column of branches into a plump cylinder, and finally into a full sphere. As you prune, step back often to look at the shape you're creating. It may take longer to fill out the bottom of the sphere than the top, especially if you're growing the myrtle in a window, since the lower branches don't receive as much light and thus grow more slowly. Be patient, and eventually the ball will round out.

As the crown gets heavier, the standard's stem will grow thicker, but a stake is still necessary, particularly when the standard is outdoors. Use a finger-thick bamboo, wood or metal stake to support a mature standard. It doesn't have to extend up through the crown, but must be at least as long as the bare stem. Always secure the stem by tying it all the way to the top of the stake. Remember that you are defying the laws of nature and gravity by balancing a ball on a stick. Countless standards have met their doom from being tied only halfway up the stem. If such a plant is jarred, the stem will sway and snap just above the highest tie. I've witnessed this disaster many times.

It will take more than two years to train a myrtle standard like this one. And at the end of that time, your work is not finished—a living plant requires constant care. To maintain a standard in prime condition, you must rotate, groom and continually prune it. You'll need to shear

back the plant every two months or so throughout its long life. Over time, the leaves will stay the same size, but there will be more and more of them as the branches grow more closely together.

After you've made a lollipop-shaped standard, you might like to experiment with creating other shapes. For a cone-shaped standard, start out by the same method as for a round-headed standard, but when the leader has reached the target height, train the branches into a cone shape. To make a double-decker (or poodle-cut) standard, again begin the same way. But this time, as the leader grows upward, leave a crown-sized (6-in. to 10-in.) section of the stem undenuded, to shape into the lower orb. Strip off the foliage below the lower tier, and between the lower and upper tiers. Prune the lower tier heavily until the leader has reached its full height, then grow both tiers out together, simultaneously pruning each to exactly the same shape. You might even try sculpting two different geometric forms on the same stem by clipping each differently. □

Tovah Martin is a houseplant specialist at Logee's Greenhouses in Danielson, Connecticut.

Once the myrtle has reached 30 in. in height, begin to shape the side branches on the top 10 in. of the stem into a spherical crown.

Standards can be trained to many shapes. Set in a protected spot outdoors where Martin works, these myrtles and other standards will grow quickly in warm, bright, summer sun. (Photo: Tovah Martin)

Pruning Shrubs

Two basic cuts control shape and growth

A close snip takes a wayward branch back to a side shoot. Thinning cuts like this control growth while preserving a natural look.

by Alan D. Cook

Pruning shrubs is a skill that combines science, art and common sense, but it's simpler than it may seem. The many different styles of pruning come from only two kinds of cuts: heading and thinning. Heading cuts shorten a branch or stem; thinning cuts remove a branch at its base or where a side branch arises. Whether you shear a hedge, whack a honey-suckle to the ground, or snip cross-wise branches and overly vigorous shoots, you'll use only two cuts.

The two kinds of cuts

To prune properly, you have to understand how a shrub grows. If untouched, shoots grow outward from their tips. Removing the tip stimulates buds lower down on the branch to grow. The buds are found at nodes, the places where leaves attach to the twig or branch. A node will have one or two (rarely three) buds, depending on the species of the shrub. Buds may be obvious or barely visible.

You make heading cuts just above nodes. The buds directly below a heading cut generally produce shoots, and often buds lower down do, too. An old rule says to cut above an outward-facing bud to encourage outward growing shoots and produce a spreading shrub. Buds that face inward may yield branches that congest the shrub or mar its shape. I sometimes ignore this rule, except on the most dominant stems, and most of my shrubs look fine.

When you make a heading cut, leave just enough of a stub to keep the buds below from drying. For a node with one bud, a slightly slanted cut is best. Put the highest point ¼-in. above the bud and the lowest point even with, and opposite, the bud. For a node with two opposite buds, cut ¼ in. above the buds at a right angle to the stem. Usually, both buds will grow, producing two equal new shoots going in opposite directions, which is often not ideal. Rub or cut off the unwanted bud, probably the inward-facing one.

Thinning cuts allow more air circulation and make branching patterns more visible. Keep the stub short when you make a thinning cut. Make the cut just above a parent or side branch, and roughly parallel to it.

If you must cut a side branch back to a larger branch or trunk, make the cut close to the larger branch at the top, and slightly farther at the bottom. If the branch to be removed is heavy, it may break away downward before the cut is cleanly accomplished, tearing off bark. So lop off the branch a foot or so above the target point and then deal with the stub.

Make clean cuts! A cut leaving torn bark and damaged wood is a bad cut, vulnerable to desiccation and attacks by insects and disease.

Why prune

I work for the Dawes Arboretum in Newark, Ohio, so I've seen most of the reasons that deciduous shrubs need pruning. Here are the most common:

To remove bad wood—Prune out any diseased, insect-infested, dead or fractured branches as soon as they're detected. Make your cuts into the healthy tissue.

To maintain a natural look—Thin out older, crowded growth and remove wayward branches. Remove suckers—new stems at the roots—and any occasional, unbranched, vertical stems; cut them at their points of origin whenever you notice them.

To train—Use heading cuts to shear hedges; thinning cuts to train espaliers to a few symmetrical branches; and both heading and thinning cuts to create topiary—shaped shrubs which require frequent maintenance pruning.

To reduce size—Reach down inside with pruners and take out the largest main stems halfway down, or even lower. Holes left will quickly fill. Then trim back the longest of the remaining branches and stems by lesser degrees. This operation has to be repeated because a too-large shrub, thus reduced, will soon be too large again.

To show attractive bark—Remove branches to open up the interior, mak-

Heading and thinning cuts
Heading and thinning cuts have different effects on subsequent growth.

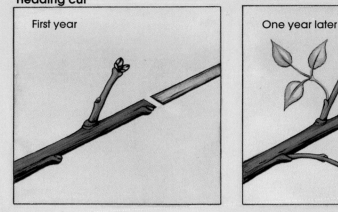

Heading cut

First year

One year later

New growth

Thinning cut

First year

One year later

New growth

How a good pruning cut should look

Correct

Bud safe from drying.

Node

Wrong

Bud may dry up.

Node

Wrong

Stub may rot.

Node

ing trunks more visible. Some shrubs, such as red-twig dogwood, have strong bark colors on young branches. They will make brilliant effects the following winter if cut to the ground before new growth begins in the spring.

To make a tree—Some large shrubs, such as viburnums, bush dogwoods, lilacs, and deciduous hollies, can become small trees with one or several

trunks if you periodically remove lower branches and weaker stems. If suckers appear, prune them away in July to minimize resuckering.

To restore old shrubs—It is possible to return tall, leggy shrubs to a more full, youthful, leafy shape by pruning, but it does take time.

There are two techniques, depending on the shrubs involved (see plant

Spring bloomers

These spring-blooming shrubs can be pruned immediately after flowering, to avoid reducing the floral display, but pruning during the winter dormant period is better for the plant.

Key: ● Shrubs with ornamental fruit, at least on some species
▲ Genera that include evergreen shrubs, which generally may be pruned in the same way as their deciduous cousins

- ▲ **Azalea**, *Rhododendron* species
- ● **Barberry**, *Berberis* species
- ●▲ **Bayberry**, *Myrica* species
- **Beautybush**, *Kolkwitzia amabilis*
- **Bigleaf hydrangea**, *Hydrangea macrophylla*
- ● **Blueberry**, highbush, *Vaccinium corymbosum*
- **Broom**, *Cytisus* species
- ● **Chokeberry**, *Aronia* species
- ●▲ **Cotoneaster**, *Cotoneaster* species
- ● **Currant**, *Ribes* species
- **Deutzia**, *Deutzia* species
- ● **Dogwood**, bush forms, *Cornus* species
- ● **Elder**, *Sambucus* species
- ●▲ **Euonymus**, *Euonymus* species
- ● **Flowering almond**, cherry, plum, *Prunus* species
- **Filbert**, *Corylus* species
- **Flowering quince**, *Chaenomeles* species
- **Forsythia**, *Forsythia* species
- **Fothergilla**, *Fothergilla* species
- ●▲ **Holly**, *Ilex* species

- ● **Honeysuckle**, *Lonicera* species
- **Jasmine**, winter, *Jasminum nudiflorum*
- ● **Jetbead**, *Rhodotypos scandens*
- **Kerria**, *Kerria japonica*
- ●▲ **Magnolia**, *Magnolia* species
- **Mock orange**, *Philadelphus* species
- **Ninebark**, *Physocarpus* species
- **Pearlbush**, *Exochorda racemosa*
- **Pea shrub**, *Caragana* species
- ●▲ **Photinia**, *Photinia* species
- **Privet**, *Ligustrum* species
- ▲ **Rhododendron**, *Rhododendron* species
- ● **Rose**, shrub types, *Rosa* species
- ● **Serviceberry**, *Amelanchier* species
- ● **Smoke tree**, *Cotinus* species
- **Snowbell**, Japanese, *Styrax japonicus*
- ● **Spicebush**, *Lindera* species
- **Spirea**, spring-blooming, *Spiraea* species
- ● **Sweet shrub**, *Calycanthus* species
- ●▲ **Viburnum**, *Viburnum* species
- **Weigela**, *Weigela florida*
- ● **White fringe** (Fringe tree), *Chionanthus* species

Summer bloomers

Summer-blooming shrubs, which flower on new growth, should be pruned in late winter or early spring, before new growth starts.

Abelia, glossy, *Abelia × grandiflora*

Aralia, five-leaf, *Acanthopanax sieboldianus*

Beautyberry, *Callicarpa* species

Bluebeard, *Caryopteris × clandonensis*

Bottlebrush buckeye, *Aesculus parviflora*

Bush cinquefoil, *Potentilla fruticosa*

Butterfly bush, *Buddleia* species, except *B. alternifolia*

Chaste tree, *Vitex* species

Coralberry, *Symphoricarpos* species

Crape myrtle, *Lagerstroemia* species

Elder, *Sambucus* species

False spirea, *Sorbaria sorbifolia*

Groundselbush, *Baccharis halimifolia*

Hydrangea, hills-of-snow, *Hydrangea arborescens* 'Grandiflora'

Hydrangea, oakleaf, *Hydrangea quercifolia*

Hydrangea, peegee, *Hydrangea paniculata* 'Grandiflora'

Japanese angelica, *Aralia elata*

Japanese spirea, *Spiraea japonica* and *S. × bumalda*

Mallow, rose, *Hibiscus moscheutos*

Rose, hybrid tea, *Rosa* species

Rose-of-Sharon (althaea), *Hibiscus syriaca*

Snowberry, *Symphoricarpos albus*

St. John's wort, *Hypericum* species

Sumac, *Rhus* species

Summer-sweet, *Clethra alnifolia*

Sweetspire, *Itea* species

---

list at right): one-shot and more gradual. The one-shot approach requires a dollop of courage. You remove every trunk, branch and twig just above ground in one raid. I attack with heavy loppers at 10 in. to 12 in., then make final cuts with a saw. If performed in summer, especially on a badly stressed shrub of an inappropriate species, this one-shot truncation can kill. Stick to late winter or early spring, and prune only healthy specimens of appropriate species.

A safer alternative to all-at-once rejuvenation is to work gradually over three years. The first year, in late winter, remove one-third of the largest old stems. The next year, take one-half of the remaining old stems. In the third year, remove the rest of the grizzled oldies. New stems will grow quickly.

Timing and tools

Horticulturists used to say, "Prune when the tools are sharp." That advice is still good when removing dead or diseased branches, but researchers have found that some times of year are ill-suited for extensive pruning. A plant's reserves of energy are highest during the dormant period of winter and lowest during spring growth. If you prune in the action weeks of spring, the shrub must draw on diminished reserves to replace at least part of the lost growth and to defend pruning wounds. Late summer and early fall are also poor times to prune—you may encourage new growth, which will fail to mature in time to withstand winter weather. Finally, avoid pruning in late fall and early winter; the wounds could stay open until spring, inviting desiccation.

The best pruning time is late winter or early spring, before buds are teased awake by warm nights. Shrubs have plenty of stored energy and are ready to grow. For shrubs that flower in spring (see chart at left), dormant pruning has a drawback. You will lose some flowers and fruits. But you'll have better growth and flowering in future years if you dormant-prune every few years and give up a few flowers and fruits.

The next best pruning time is in early summer, after all or nearly all foliage has matured, when only the last bits of immature growth are still evident—roughly the first two weeks of July here in central Ohio. Wait for a day when foliage is dry, especially if diseases such as mildew or fire blight are evident. Summer pruning reduces vigor, because it removes more leaves than can grow back in one year.

Pruning tools must be sharp, steel-wool clean, and suited to the job at hand. My three indispensable tools for pruning shrubs are a sturdy pair of hand shears with scissors action; loppers with the capacity to cut stems at least 1½ in. in diameter; and a seven-teeth-to-the-inch pruning saw with a cutting edge of 8 in.

Keep tools clean and sharp. Use kerosene or WD-40 to clean away sap and pitch. Sharpen scissors-type pruning shear blades on outside curved sides only. Take saws to a professional sharpener.

I recommend you avoid power tools for pruning, except for electric hedge shears. Chain saws are for full time professional tree people, not for week-end amateur shrub people.

Some do and don't advice

Remember a hair-cutting adage—"You can't put it back." Take off a bit, step back, look; you can always go at it again if necessary.

Come back on periodic inspection visits to see whether your pruning is doing the job you wanted. You can learn from successes and failures, and often you can correct the latter.

Toss small prunings into a basket or onto a tarp for easy clean-up. Place larger branches with butt ends together, for the same efficiency.

Forget wound dressing. It used to be common practice to paint large cut areas. Recent research shows it does no good, and occasionally even encourages disease organisms.

"Don't prune when the temperature is below 20°F." I read this somewhere, and treat it as gospel—I can sit by the fire and wait for warmer winter weather before I shape my plants. □

Alan D. Cook is Director of Extended Services at the Dawes Arboretum in Newark, Ohio.

How to reduce an overgrown shrub
Wrong

First year

One year later — New growth

Correct

First year

One year later — New growth

Drastic rejuvenation
Some overgrown shrubs can be renewed by cutting back drastically.

Before

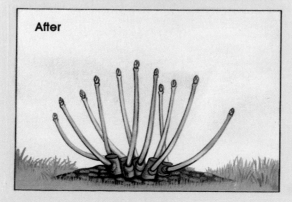
After

Pruning Trees
Make the kindest cut

by Alex L. Shigo

When you remove a branch, the tree must defend an open wound. Whether the outcome is health or decay depends on how you cut. If you prune properly, the tree can readily cope with the injury. If you prune improperly, you threaten the tree's health.

Trees respond to injury by isolating the damage. They do not heal, as people do, by regenerating damaged tissues. Instead, they sacrifice injured wood to protect the healthy. In the vicinity of a wound, trees activate living cells that store oils, starches and other materials. The cells convert their stores into compounds that coalesce around the wound, forming boundaries that restrict the spread of pathogens and insects. The isolated wood dies, but the rest of the tree lives on.

Proper pruning cuts and improper pruning cuts have different outcomes because trees do not produce uniform defenses. While they strongly resist the spread of pathogens and insects across growth rings and across the radial sheets of cells called rays (see the drawing on the facing page), they offer less resistance in the axis of sap flow. When conductive tissues are injured, as they are by improper pruning, rot tends to spread farther above and below the wound than it does to the sides or into the tree. Trees have another defensive zone at the base of branches, where they form a boundary that markedly inhibits the spread of pathogens. Proper pruning preserves the tissues where this protective barrier forms and does not injure conductive tissues.

Times to prune
Energy reserves are the fuel of a tree's defense system. When the cells have ample reserves, the tree forms strong barriers against pests and diseases. If the reserves are low, the barriers are weak.

A tree's energy reserves increase and

Built-in defenses keep rot and insects from invading a tree after pruning, provided the collar-like bulge at the branch base is intact.

decrease in an annual cycle. The fine roots start absorbing water and elements in late winter, often with snow still on the ground. Then the tips of the twigs awaken and the buds begin to open. Once the leaves have opened, new wood begins to form in the branches, and then in the trunk. During these phases, the tree draws mainly on stored energy to fuel its growth. By the time leaves have formed, reserves are usually at their lowest. Then, within days, the new leaves begin trapping the sun's energy and the reserves increase rapidly.

I feel strongly that the best time to prune is when the tree has the greatest reserves and is ready to grow. That means during late dormancy, before buds begin to swell. If need be, you can also prune during most of the growing season, but wait until a few weeks after the leaves have opened. The worst times to prune are when leaves are forming, because reserves are low, and when leaves are falling, because new absorption roots develop then and pruning drains energy that would have gone into their formation.

You should also refrain from pruning living branches when you believe for oth-

er reasons that a tree has low reserves—during or after a season of severe drought, if the tree has lost a considerable number of leaves to disease or pests, or if it has been harshly pruned in the last few years. Under these circumstances, prune in a year or two, when the tree can defend itself more aggressively. Pruning living branches from a weakened tree invites disaster. Do remove any branch that is waning or dead, regardless of the season or the tree's condition.

The branch collar
In 26 years of research for the U.S. Forest Service, I pruned thousands of branches on many different species of trees, then returned to the trees later (years later in many cases), felled them, and chainsawed the trunks longitudinally through the various pruning cuts to study the trees' defenses. The results were conclusive. Pruning a branch by cutting it flush with the trunk or branch it arises from forces the tree to sacrifice large reserves of energy and considerable amounts of wood. Unfortunately, some tree-care professionals and many books on pruning still advocate making flush pruning cuts.

The key to proper pruning is a distinctive bulge at the base of a branch. The wood at the base of a branch is made up of a series of collars (see the bottom drawing on the facing page). In early spring, each branch adds a layer of tissues that circle the branch base to form a collar. Later, after leaves develop, the trunk adds a layer of tissues that circle the new branch collar. (I'll call the whole system collectively the branch collar.) This interlocking system is the most wondrous natural phenomenon I have ever seen. A branch has extraordinary strength and resiliency, and yet it is not one piece with the tree. If you pull a three- or four-year-old branch off with a downward tug, you can actually feel the collars popping past each other.

The kindest cut
When you prune a branch, leave the branch collar intact. That is nature's meth-

Photo above: Staff; all other photos: **Alex L. Shigo**

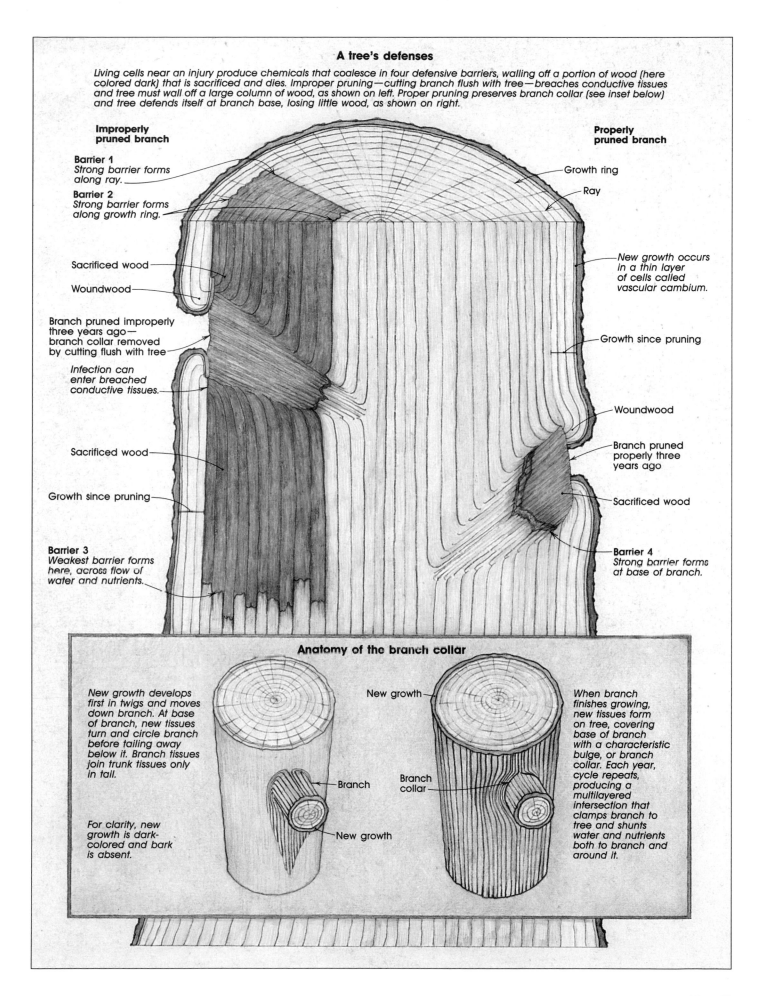

A tree's defenses

Living cells near an injury produce chemicals that coalesce in four defensive barriers, walling off a portion of wood (here colored dark) that is sacrificed and dies. Improper pruning—cutting branch flush with tree—breaches conductive tissues and tree must wall off a large column of wood, as shown on left. Proper pruning preserves branch collar (see inset below) and tree defends itself at branch base, losing little wood, as shown on right.

Improperly pruned branch

Barrier 1
Strong barrier forms along ray.

Barrier 2
Strong barrier forms along growth ring.

Sacrificed wood

Woundwood

Branch pruned improperly three years ago— branch collar removed by cutting flush with tree

Infection can enter breached conductive tissues.

Sacrificed wood

Growth since pruning

Barrier 3
Weakest barrier forms here, across flow of water and nutrients.

Properly pruned branch

Growth ring

Ray

New growth occurs in a thin layer of cells called vascular cambium.

Growth since pruning

Woundwood

Branch pruned properly three years ago

Sacrificed wood

Barrier 4
Strong barrier forms at base of branch.

Anatomy of the branch collar

New growth develops first in twigs and moves down branch. At base of branch, new tissues turn and circle branch before tailing away below it. Branch tissues join trunk tissues only in tail.

For clarity, new growth is dark-colored and bark is absent.

New growth

Branch

New growth

New growth

Branch collar

When branch finishes growing, new tissues form on tree, covering base of branch with a characteristic bulge, or branch collar. Each year, cycle repeats, producing a multilayered intersection that clamps branch to tree and shunts water and nutrients both to branch and around it.

Illustrations: Laura B. Goodwin

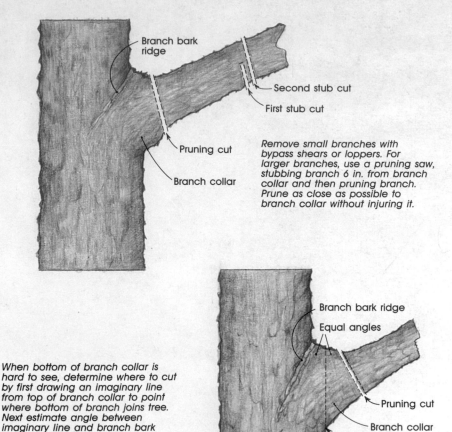

Branch bark ridge

Second stub cut

First stub cut

Pruning cut

Branch collar

Remove small branches with bypass shears or loppers. For larger branches, use a pruning saw, stubbing branch 6 in. from branch collar and then pruning branch. Prune as close as possible to branch collar without injuring it.

Branch bark ridge

Equal angles

Pruning cut

Branch collar

Imaginary line

When bottom of branch collar is hard to see, determine where to cut by first drawing an imaginary line from top of branch collar to point where bottom of branch joins tree. Next estimate angle between imaginary line and branch bark ridge. Then cut branch at same angle. Start cut alongside top of branch collar.

The results of proper and improper pruning
The author pruned thousands of trees, some properly, some improperly, and observed the aftermath. Here he has sliced longitudinally through portions of two trees, several years after pruning a branch from each. On the right, a flush cut removed the branch collar and led to extensive rot in the tree, visible as columns of pale blotchy wood above and below the wound that extend beyond the sections shown here. A crack has developed at the base of the wound, where the bark has turned under, separating new wood from old. Improper pruning often produces lengthy cracks above and below wounds. On the left, proper pruning left the branch collar intact, and the tree has walled off the base of the branch, confining rot to two small discolored areas at the edge of the wound. New wood is growing over the old without producing cracks.

od, when branches wane from injury, lack of light, or attack by insects and pathogens. The tree forms a protective barrier inside the branch collar, and the branch rots and falls off, leaving the branch collar intact. Pruning cuts that breach or eliminate the collar destroy the branch protection zone and cut through the interlocking tissues of the collar, leaving conductive tissues open to invasion and infection.

The proper pruning cut starts from the top of the branch collar and ends at its bottom (see the drawing at left). If you take a few minutes to stroll around your neighborhood and look at branch collars, you'll learn that they vary widely. On some species they are thick and prominent; on others they are flat and close to the trunk. Conifers, for example, frequently have nearly flat branch collars. The variations in collars mean that there is no set location or angle for a proper pruning cut. You may cut one branch ½ in. from the trunk and almost vertically, and another branch 4 in. from the trunk and 30° off vertical. What determines a proper cut is the position of the branch collar.

Before sawing larger branches off at the branch collar, shorten them to 6-in. stubs. If you omit this precaution, the branch is liable to tear away from the tree as you near the end of the pruning cut, ripping out the tissues at the bottom of the branch collar and below. Make the initial stub cut on the underside of the branch, 6 in. from the branch collar and about a third of the way through the branch. Start the second stub cut on the top of the branch, outboard from the first cut and ¼ in. or less away from it. Be prepared for the branch to break away suddenly as you near the first cut. Once the branch falls, make the proper pruning cut at the branch collar, removing the stub.

With thick or highly prominent branch collars, many people hesitate to prune properly. They feel that preserving the branch collar leaves the tree with an unsightly volcanolike wound. The temptation to cut through the branch collar is greater still when a branch has been dead for some years and the branch collar has grown like a sleeve around it. On large dying and dead branches, the branch collar may grow outward several feet. But no matter how prominent the branch collar, leave it intact.

Conversely, don't try to safeguard the branch collar by cutting the branch an inch away. Branch stubs are like buffets for pathogens and insects, and once an infestation has gathered strength in a branch stub, it may push past the base of the branch and get into the tree. Proper pruning does not leave a stub.

Branch bark ridge—The branch bark ridge is raised bark between a branch and the trunk. As the tree grows, the raised bark persists on the trunk in a line to each side of the branch. Never cut behind the branch bark ridge. If you have trouble distinguishing the branch collar, you can make a proper pruning cut by taking an angle that mirrors the angle between the branch bark ridge and the trunk (see the drawing on the facing page).

When a branch is not a branch—Trees fork as well as branch. In pruning, the difference matters. When a tree forks, the result is two codominant stems, each connected to half the stem below. Removing a codominant stem opens half the stem below to pests and diseases. What's more, codominant stems have no built-in defense zone as branches do. When they are pruned, the tree struggles to wall off the injury.

The goal in pruning a codominant stem is to make a wound the tree can defend and eventually close. As with branches, the proper cut varies. But codominant stems do not form branch collars, so take your pruning indications from the stem bark ridge (see the top photo at far right). The cut should start beside the top of the stem bark ridge and end directly across from the bottom of the ridge.

Safety first—I recommend that you prune only what you can reach with hand tools while standing on the ground. Don't work on a ladder and don't climb. For small branches, use sharp bypass shears. They work closer to the branch collar than anvil shears do. For somewhat larger branches, use bypass loppers, and for bigger branches, use a sharp pruning saw. Leave chain saws for the professionals. When the job is too big, hire a tree-care professional—an arborist—who understands proper pruning.

After pruning

In the years after you prune a branch, the branch collar grows over the wound, laying down new wood. First the wound produces callus, which is tissue that is not woody and that can generate buds and sprouts. Then the callus produces woundwood, which is woody and does not form buds. On properly made cuts, the woundwood advances evenly (see the bottom photo at far right). If woundwood fails to grow at the top or bottom of the wound, or grows slowly in those places, it's a sure sign that the pruning cut injured the branch collar. On improper cuts—cuts through the branch collar, or flush with the tree—the woundwood may curl under on itself and grow bark between it and the tree, starting a permanent crack. Even if the wound eventually closes, the flaw remains. Years later, when stress splits the bark, the damage is blamed on frost. No one remembers the pruning mistake.

Don't confuse the growth of wound-

Codominant stems

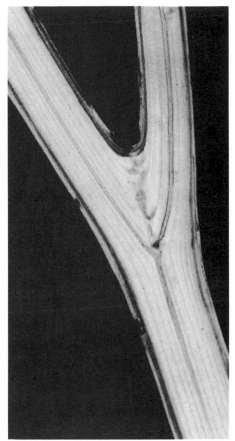

Codominant stems differ from branches in several ways: they have roughly equal girth, are each continuous with the half of the stem below them, and lack branch collars (left). Pruning a codominant stem usually forces the tree to wall off and sacrifice more wood than pruning a branch does. The proper pruning cut (above) starts at the top of the stem bark ridge and ends opposite the end of the stem bark ridge.

Woundwood

New growth slowly closes pruning wounds. When a branch is properly pruned, the new growth advances evenly around the wound. The photo at right shows the development of woundwood several years after proper pruning. On a flush cut, new growth often first advances only at the sides of the wound, a sure sign that tissues have died above and below the wound, as shown above.

wood with healing. It's a common misconception, and it leads to disaster. It happens that cutting the branch collar usually produces fast-growing woodwood. You can see what comes next— people cut off the branch collar to speed up the woodwood. A tree's injuries never "heal." The tree carries them all its life, safely walled off, if all goes well.

Wound dressings—The concept of wound dressings, like the idea of healing, confuses trees with people. The analogy seems to be that a cut finger needs disinfectant, so a tree wound needs dressing. Over the centuries, innumerable dressings have been concocted, purported to protect trees by barring fungal infections and insect pests. For years, I assumed they worked. Then I began testing them to see which worked best. To my surprise, I eventually found that none had beneficial effects, and what's worse, some actually encouraged pathogens and insect pests. My experiments were straightforward. I pruned branches that were much alike, then dressed half the wounds and left the other half alone. After seven years, there were few differences between the two groups. The trees had isolated and closed most wounds alike. Wound dressings actually harmed some trees, however, such as white oaks, which had more decay than trees with untreated wounds. The experiments changed my mind about wound dressings. If branches are pruned properly, pathogens seldom spread into the tree. If branches are pruned improperly, no dressing will keep pathogens out.

Nature has a wound dressing that resists pathogens. It is the compounds that surround injuries. What we must not do is destroy the only wound dressing that works!

Occasions for pruning

As a general rule, restrict pruning to branches that endanger the health of the tree (see the examples on the facing page). These branches fall into several categories. The easiest to spot are dead, dying or infested branches. Remove them as soon as you see them. The remaining categories cover branches that may eventually fall from their own weight, injuring the tree and endangering people.

Some branches squeeze so tightly against the tree or an adjacent branch that bark is trapped in the crotch year after year, interrupting and weakening the branch collar. The condition is called included bark. As the branch gains weight, it may pull away from the tree, opening a crack along the included bark. Eventually, the branch will tear away from the tree.

Learn to spot included bark, and prune the affected branch as early as possible. Branches that ascend from the tree at a steep angle, and codominant stems that grow close together, often develop included bark. So do branches that arise from the tree too close together. Check them. If there is no ridge of bark in the crotch between branch and tree, or in the crotch between codominant stems, you must prune. Start the cut at the bottom of the branch collar, not the top, and cut upward, ending as close to the tree as you can. This is tricky work, and no matter how well you do it, the tree must sacrifice a considerable amount of wood to wall off the wound.

Another sort of weak branch arises from the tree later than—often years later than—neighboring branches. It is called an epicormic branch, meaning "on the trunk," and develops either from a dormant bud that has persisted for many years or from a new bud formed in the callus that follows injury. Shortening large branches—a misguided practice called topping—often provokes the development of epicormic branches. The epicormic branches grow larger while decay spreads below them. Eventually the branches may tear away from the tree. Epicormic branches can also develop from unwounded portions of a tree, and often do when a tree has been overpruned. Most of them are weakly attached to the tree. They grow much like branches that develop included bark. If many epicormic sprouts form, remove the smaller, weaker ones only.

An old tree that has grown all its life in the company of other trees may develop dangerous branches when some of the neighboring trees are removed. As its branches grow into the vacancy, they may get so heavy that they fall off, particularly if they have old wounds near their bases. If you see cracks at the base of suspect branches, ask a professional to look.

REFERENCES

The author has published two books about tree growth and tree care. Both are hardcover, printed on coated paper, and copiously illustrated with photos and drawings. They are available mail-order from Shigo and Trees, Associates, 4 Denbow Rd., Durham, NH 03284.

The New Tree Biology, 1986, 612 pp., $55.00 postpaid. Written principally for tree-care professionals, but scientifically minded gardeners will gain a deep appreciation of tree growth.

Tree Pruning, 1989, 192 pp., $42.00 postpaid. A guide to proper pruning. Not for doing it yourself, except in limited cases, but valuable for using a tree professional knowledgeably.

Training a tree

Pruning from the early stages of a tree's life is the best way to assure the tree's health, size and safety. Removing branches early is far safer for the tree than removing them years later. It is also the only good way to control the size and shape of a tree. You cannot prune a big tree to make it a small healthy tree. You can, however, keep a small tree a small healthy tree for a long time by proper pruning. If you are pruning for convenience—to make mowing easier around a tree in the lawn, or to limit the size of a tree near your house to preserve a view—start early.

Prune young trees carefully. You'll find that their branch collars tend to be quite prominent. Left intact on a slender trunk, they look unsightly to some people. Nevertheless, don't be tempted to remove them. Also avoid pruning several branches that are close together. Prune one branch, then wait a year or two before removing another.

When you buy young trees at a nursery, look closely for signs of poor pruning. Many nurseries, unfortunately, remove branch collars for cosmetic reasons. You'll see woundwood on the sides but not the top or bottom of flush cuts. You may also see a sunken spot above the cut, which indicates damage in the trunk. On some species, such as lindens and elms, you may see sprouts around the wound. When you prune the sprouts, more will appear. Some nurseries let young trees grow with low branches because the extra photosynthesis increases the diameter of the trunk. When sale time is near, the low branches are pruned, which produces closely packed wounds. Avoid these trees.

Responsibility

The single most important step you can take to keep a tree healthy is not pruning but rather planting it in the right place. People insist on planting trees where they should not—hemlocks in front of picture windows, for example, or eucalyptus trees under power lines. Then when the trees are too big, whack! they are topped and die a slow death. Trees should die with dignity. If a large tree has to be topped, it is better to remove it. When you plant trees that can outgrow their site, start pruning them early.

We are responsible for trees. I believe what the fox said in Antoine de Saint-Exupery's *The Little Prince:* "Men have forgotten this truth. But you must not forget it. You become responsible, forever, for what you have tamed." □

Since retiring from the U.S. Forest Service in 1985, Alex L. Shigo has made a new career of educating people about trees. He lives in Durham, New Hampshire.

Occasions to prune

The three sorts of branches shown here threaten the health of a tree, and should be pruned as early as possible. Dying and dead branches (photo below) are havens for insects and rot. Branches with included bark (center photos) can tear away from the tree under their own weight. Epicormic branches (photos at far right), which develop around wounds or after heavy pruning, can also be hazardous.

Dying and dead branches—Remove promptly. If a branch has been dead for several years, the branch collar may have grown outward. Nonetheless, preserve it, as shown here.

Included bark—Branches that grow close to the tree may develop included bark, which interrupts and weakens the branch collar (above). The outward sign of included bark is the absence of a branch bark ridge in the crotch (at top). Prune by cutting upward, starting at the bottom of the branch collar and ending as close as possible to the tree.

Epicormic branches—Epicormic branches develop when buds that have been carried in the cambium begin to grow, as shown at top, or when new buds form and sprout in the tissues around wounds, like the improper pruning cut above. Epicormic branches are often weakly attached to the tree, due to included bark, and should be removed while small.

Don't top

Don't try to reduce a tree's size by cutting back large branches between limbs, a practice called topping. Topping produces decay and hazardous sprouts. Only early training can control tree size safely. Trees too large for their site should be removed.

Topping—Cutting back large branches, or topping, causes epicormic branches to sprout profusely around the wound. Meanwhile, rot spreads below the wound; note the hole in the tree at right and the decay in the halved branch and sprouts at far right. Weakly attached, the sprouts around topping cuts are prone to tear away from the tree as they gain in size.

Shaping a Pine Tree

A traditional Japanese pruning technique creates a picturesque tree

A traditional Japanese technique for pruning pines gives them the look of gnarled old trees growing in the mountains, lending a feeling of permanence to a garden. Author Slawson demonstrates these techniques with this Scots pine growing in a garden he designed at Carleton College in Northfield, Minnesota.

by David Slawson

For more than a thousand years, Japanese gardeners (and before them, the Chinese) have transplanted gnarled old pines from the mountains into their gardens. Each year, they selectively prune off branches, pinch back new springtime growth and remove old needles from these trees in order to maintain and to heighten their appearance. These trees afford viewers, in the comfort of their own gardens, the sublime feelings associated with faraway craggy mountains.

Mature trees are still sometimes dug from the wild today in Japan, but more often young pines are painstakingly pruned in the nursery and then pruned and pinched annually to resemble much older-looking specimens. I think these traditional Japanese techniques can be used by American gardeners to great effect to evoke the feeling of a mountain or hillside habitat, and so recall our ancient longings for the ethereal quality of a pristine wilderness. A gnarled pine lends a sense of timelessness to a garden. Selective pruning reveals the trunk and branch structure, and allows the landscape beyond to come into view. Pinching back the new growth in the spring produces a fluffy, delicate effect when the new needles emerge. Removing dead, brown needles in the autumn gives the tree a fresh, green appearance for winter, enhancing its contrast with dreary winter skies.

Pruning in this manner does more than add beauty to a garden. Once the tree is opened up and dead needles are removed, more light and air penetrate the canopy. Careful pruning is also a rich experience for the gardener. As I stand or crouch close to one of these trees, I'm aware of the play of the wind sighing through the needles and of their fresh, pungent scent, immersing my spirit in a rarified atmosphere.

I learned this pruning technique in Japan as an apprentice to Kinsaku Nakane, a renowned master of the art. While I can't communicate all the nuances in a magazine article, I can get you started. One of the best ways to get the hang of this type of pruning is to study ancient pines or other conifers. In the mountains, look for those most exposed to the ele-

Photos: above, David Slawson; all others: Staff

ments. You're also likely to find mature trees near old farmhouses, in cemeteries or in open fields. Chinese and Japanese landscape paintings of gnarled pines will provide inspiration as well. As the famous haiku poet Basho once said, "Go to the pine if you want to learn about the pine."

The process starts with reflection rather than action. Consider how the form of the tree fits into the garden, as well as how the garden fits into the surrounding landscape. For example, the pine in the photos here is in a garden that I designed at Carleton College in Northfield, Minnesota. In this landscape, I wanted to evoke the nearby rolling hills and bluffs and the undulating greenery bordering the Minnesota River, much as a traditional garden in Japan might evoke mountains and fast-flowing streams. The pine is one of many elements in the garden. I positioned it to be viewed from a sitting pavilion. Seen from there, it visually balances a group of rocks that suggest a mountainous outcropping. Looking up from the bench, the viewer sees the sky filtered through the needles and branches of the tree. There are other evergreens in the garden, and the pine contrasts with their textures and shapes. As I prune the pine, I keep these and other relationships in mind.

Pruning for structure

To create a gnarled, ancient-looking pine, look for a tree with an interesting branch structure. This may be a tree in a nursery or one already on your property. Most often these trees will have been sheared into the conical shape so popular in this country; some may have been left untended. Sheared or unsheared, a pine's beautiful trunk and branch structure can be retrieved. Young trees are more malleable, but even an older pine can be thinned. As you examine a candidate, attune to the tree's inherent nature. Put on gloves and penetrate the thick foliage about two-thirds of the way up the tree. Gently move the branches aside and look for a diagonally leaning trunk or one with a crook and some twisting branches. If you decide to purchase the tree, prune out the excess branches while you're still at the nursery (with the nursery person's permission). You can prune out as much as one-third of the total growth. A pruned pine is easier to transport, less liable to be damaged or to dry out during the move, and easier to position properly in the garden.

When pruning, start by viewing the heart of the tree from all angles. (I find it useful to mentally divide the tree from top to bottom into the head, the heart and the trunk, approximately corresponding to the upper quarter, midquarter and lower half, respectively. Most of the branches in the head grow vertically and diagonally, while those below tend to grow horizon-

The new growth of a pine—the candles—projects upward from the branch ends. Pinching back the candles produces delicate new growth.

tally.) Focus your attention on the front of the tree, the part that looks most pleasing to you, the part whose lines you'll want to choreograph with other garden elements. You'll know the front as surely as you know this is the tree for you, and you'll naturally orient yourself to it, just as you do when you face a friend with whom you're talking.

Working from the front, prune out any vertical branches that visually compete with and crowd the trunk. Use sharp pruning shears, don't cut the branch collar and don't leave stubs. (See the article on pp. 54-59 for more on pruning trees.) Then prune out any branches that crowd, cross or rub against the more gnarled, outward-stretching branches. If a branch is straight or otherwise lacking in character, remove it. Where two branches run parallel and close to each other, remove the least picturesque one, or partially trim one of them back, as described in the next paragraph. Where multiple branches radiate from the trunk at nearly the same height, prune out all but three or four so their spacing is well balanced. Once you've thinned to reveal the heart of the tree, do the same with the head and then the trunk. The resulting trunk and branching pattern should appear natural and not imposed; spare and yet expressive, like a dancer's pose.

After you've completely removed entire branches to open up the tree, you should also trim off some of the straighter, longer branches to places where they become gnarled and more sculptural, a procedure called heading back. Always prune back to a lateral branch, never between branches. Head back some branches more than others. If you want either the entire tree or a particular branch to grow larger, don't head it back until it has reached the desired size. Removing and

heading back branches establishes the structure of the tree. Each autumn, you'll need to prune selectively to maintain this look and to keep the tree open.

While you prune, think of yourself as a sculptor, releasing a figure from an uncarved granite block. Pruning is an all-involving, empathetic activity. Let the tree speak to you, rather than imposing your will on it. Step back and look at the whole tree. Some of the branches will look as if they belong there, part of the enduring form that would develop in old age. Remove those that detract from that form. As you remove branches from the tree, its inherent beauty and character gradually will be revealed. The billowy wreath of greenery on the ends of the outer branches will softly frame the sharp, sinuous lines of the inner branches and trunk. Seen through this window of needles, the tree gains depth, a quality that's enhanced by the contrast between the green foliage and the reddish-brown or gray-black pine bark. When sunlight filters through the branches, the bark glows against the soft green of the needles.

Pinching candles

Each spring, long slender shoots, called candles, grow from buds at the end of each branch. These buff-colored candles are covered with prickly bumps, from which new needles emerge. Latent buds lie in the axils at the base of the new needles, ready to sprout if the end of the candle is damaged or pinched back. As the tree matures, the candles become branches. Eventually some of these limbs die and break off, revealing the tree's structure.

By pinching back new candles in the spring, you can stimulate more candle formation within a smaller area, as well as control the tree's size. When needles on the closely clustered candles fill in, they form billowy layers, making a young tree look more ancient. The best time to pinch is when the candles are about 3 in. to 4 in. long and still tender and pliable, and the needles are just beginning to emerge. Timing varies with location; it's mid- to late May in southern Minnesota. Don't wait until the candles harden so much that you can't easily pinch them off—far fewer buds will sprout and you're liable to damage those that have formed.

There are usually many new candles at the end of each branch. Most of them grow outward away from the trunk, but some grow in toward the trunk. If you pinch all the candles partway back, the resulting growth at the end of the branch will become too dense. So, first completely remove some of the candles, leaving an average of five at the end of each branch, three pointing outward and two inward. This ratio of 3:2 corresponds to the pine's natural growth habit. Leave more if you want the tree to grow bush-

Removing candles

In spring, remove some candles from each branch, leaving a ratio of three pointing outward to two inward.

Candle

In the spring, when new candles are still pliable, Slawson completely removes some by snapping them off at the base. He aims to leave a ratio of three facing outward from the trunk to two facing inward.

for this order. The top of a young tree grows most vigorously, so it must be thinned and pinched back most heavily. By starting at the top, you'll avoid dropping candles on the part you've already completed, making it easier to see what you've done. And it's more efficient to complete each branch before moving on to the next one. The Japanese describe the top of the tree as yang, representing the active, revealed part of the tree's "coiled dragonlike" force, and the bottom part of the tree as yin, outwardly soft, concealed and full of possibilities. The yang portion must be contained more than the yin, which can be allowed to spread into a widening span of denser branches.

To pinch back a candle, grasp it between your thumb and forefinger at the point you want to remove it and gently bend it sideways until it snaps off. The length of the candles should be in scale with the size of the tree—very long candles would look incongruous on a small tree. As a rule of thumb, if the candle is new and very pliable, break off one-third to one-half or more of its length. If the candle is stiffer (and therefore older and longer), break off two-thirds or more. Within these guidelines, vary the lengths of candles on the same branch. Don't worry about being too precise; just relax

ier—as many as five pointing outward and three inward. If you want a sparser look, leave as few as two pointing out and one in. (If you want the tree to get larger, thin the candles but don't pinch them back until the tree has reached the desired size.) Remove the largest candle, particularly if it's the one growing in a straight line with the branch from which it arises. This will encourage a zigzag

branching pattern. Don't remove two adjacent candles or all the inward-facing ones—that would leave an unsightly space. To completely remove a candle, just snap it off at the base between your thumb and forefinger.

First thin, and then pinch, the candles on each branch, starting at the top of the tree and working your way down. There are practical and philosophical reasons

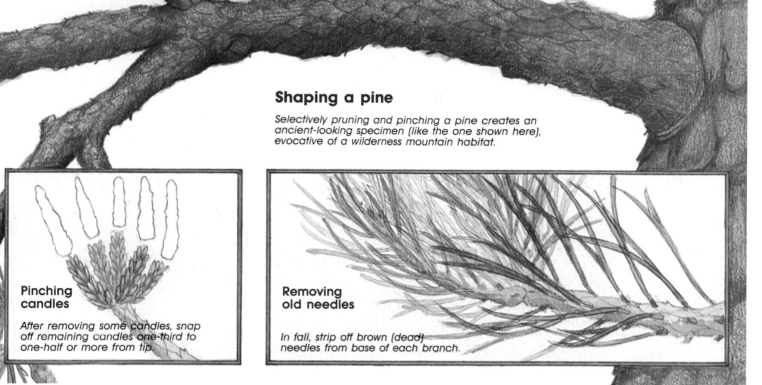

Shaping a pine

Selectively pruning and pinching a pine creates an ancient-looking specimen (like the one shown here), evocative of a wilderness mountain habitat.

Pinching candles

After removing some candles, snap off remaining candles one-third to one-half or more from tip.

Removing old needles

In fall, strip off brown (dead) needles from base of each branch.

and let your eye become the judge, looking at the tree from different perspectives.

In the succeeding weeks, the needles will grow out and the tree will have a fluffy, full-foliage look to complement the trunk and branching structure. The full effect of pinching back the candles will be realized after just two or three years. If you want to get a more delicate quality even sooner, you can totally pinch off all the candles as soon as they've formed. This stimulates a second flush of candles, weaker than the first, which then can be thinned and pinched as described above.

Pinching candles doesn't take as long as you might think. For example, the 12-ft. Scots pine at Carleton required about two full days, not an unreasonable amount of time to spend for such a striking effect. You can spread out the work over several days or even a couple of weekends, as long as the candles are still pliable enough. Pinching the candles in the early light of day or in the late afternoon is a meditative way to spend time outdoors.

Removing old needles

After several years, a pine needle dies, turns brown and drops from the tree during the winter. Removing dead needles in the fall gives the pine a radiant look through the winter. (The needles can be

After removing some candles, Slawson pinches the rest partway back. Grasping the length he wants to remove between his thumb and forefinger, he bends it sideways until it breaks off.

taken off in early spring, if need be.) Grab the base of each little branch between the thumb and forefinger of both hands. Keep one hand in place and carefully run the thumb and forefinger of your other hand from the base of the branch toward its tip, stripping off the brown needles as you go with a gentle, even pressure. They come off the stem easily. Stop when you reach live, green

needles. Be careful not to injure the tiny buds for next year's growth, which have already formed in the needle axils. ☐

David Slawson is a landscape designer living in Almo, Kentucky, and author of Secret Teachings in the Art of Japanese Gardens: Design Principles, Aesthetic Values (Kodansha International, 114 Fifth Ave., New York, NY 10011; 1987; $34.95).

Illustration: Laura B. Goodwin

Deadheading and Cutting Back

More flowers and neater growth

By removing spent flowers, the author encourages her cheery 'Summer Sun' heliopsis to keep blooming. Prompt deadheading stretches its bloom period from June through September and checks its rampant self-seeding.

All photos: Staff

by Tracy DiSabato-Aust

Y**ou** might associate pruning with woody plants, but pruning also benefits herbaceous perennials and annuals. When you deadhead spent flowers, cut back leggy plants, pinch stems or disbud, you are actually pruning. Timely trimming of herbaceous plants promotes compact growth, prolonged bloom, larger flowers and more luxuriant foliage. It even facilitates autumn clean-up in the garden. Deadheading and cutting back should be regular chores in an ornamental garden. But you'll disbud only if you're after show plants, like dahlias, with a few large flowers, and you'll pinch only to keep annuals compact or to delay bloom in autumn-flowering perennials like chrysanthemums.

Deadheading is simply removing faded and spent flowers. It improves a plant's appearance and may prolong the blooming period or initiate a second flush of bloom. On plants like Shasta daisy and yarrow, which have foliage on the flower stems, deadhead spent flowers by cutting them off just above the foliage or along the stem just above new flower buds. For spring-flowering bulbs, hostas and daylilies, which have leafless flower stems, cut their spent stems close to the ground.

Deadheading also prevents self-seeding, but you may choose to leave the seed heads in order to have new plants next year or to add visual interest to your winter garden. Some widely grown plants with attractive seed heads include Sedum 'Autumn Joy', globe thistle, purple coneflower, and rudbeckia. In my garden, I allow annuals, perennials and biennials, including columbine, love-in-a-mist (*Nigella damascena*) and foxglove, to self-sow, creating an unplanned, cottage-garden look. Love-in-a-mist has attractive seed heads that I use in dried flower arrangements, another reason I leave some plants to reseed.

Pinching is removing the growing tips of a plant, usually just above the uppermost full set of leaves. In reaction, the plant produces new branches, grows bushy and compact, and flowers later. Pinched plants also produce more, but smaller, flowers than unpinched ones. Late-summer

and autumn-flowering plants, such as asters and chrysanthemums, benefit most from pinching.

Disbudding is the removal of flower buds. If side buds are removed, a plant's terminal bud will produce one large flower on a long stem. If the terminal bud is removed, side shoots will produce many small flowers. Disbudding is used mostly on plants such as chrysanthemums, dahlias, carnations and peonies grown for show.

Cutting back means pruning a plant uniformly to reduce its height, renew its appearance or encourage a new flush of growth and flowering. Cut back plants that have grown leggy from too much shade or fertilizer to make them grow more compactly. Bloomed-out perennials as well as annuals and herbs that take on a rangy, sunburned appearance in midsummer will produce new growth and often bloom again if cut back.

Which technique you use depends on the plant, the timing and what you want. I'll explain your choices for several broad groups of garden plants—ornamental grasses, herbaceous perennials or annuals. If you have questions about a plant, check "Timetable for Pruning Herbaceous Plants," pp. 66-67

Spring-flowering perennials—Cut back low-growing rock garden or edging plants by half after they've bloomed to keep them compact and to promote growth. Pruners are the best tool for cutting back small plantings, but I do landscape contracting, and I use a string trimmer in large beds and on ground covers to speed this labor-intensive chore. String trimmers have the disadvantage of cutting less cleanly than pruners, but I find that the plants fill in rapidly.

Deadhead spring-flowering plants such as bleeding-heart 'Luxuriant' and peach-leaved bellflower (*Campanula persicifolia*). Many gardeners make the mistake of cutting bellflower back instead of deadheading, thereby losing flower buds. To avoid this pitfall, look for the tiny buds that hide in bellflower's leaf axils, and then cut just above them. Columbines are heavy seeders, so if you don't want them everywhere, deadhead before seeds set. To keep these plants tidy, prune the leaves as they yellow.

Spring-flowering bulbs gone to seed are unattractive and lose their vigor. Prune the bloomed-out flower stalks at the base of the plant. Let the plant's

leaves remain until they yellow, though, because they manufacture food for the next season's flowers. When the foliage dies, you can cut it off at the base, but I find it easier to pull it by hand because it comes away from the bulb cleanly.

Summer-flowering perennials—Summer is the busiest time for deadheading and other pruning chores. Many perennials, including yarrow, salvia and heliopsis, ordinarily have one strong flowering. I find that salvia will have a second flush of bloom if deadheaded, and the yarrows can bloom two and even three times if deadheaded regularly. Some plants, like lanceleaf tickseed (*Coreopsis lanceolata*) and most daylilies, require daily deadheading. Phlox will produce flowering side branches if the bloomed-out main panicle, or flower cluster, is removed. I've had phlox 'Alpha' and 'Miss Lingard' bloom in June and then flower again in August. Deadheading phlox also prevents seeding and overcrowding.

Delphiniums benefit from various forms of pruning. I deadhead them from the time they first flower in June and early July, until they stop blooming in late July. Later, usually the first or second week in August, I cut the plant back to the new growth at its base and get a second flush of bloom in September. If you want larger flowers, remove a third of the delphinium stems early in spring.

Biennials such as foxglove and sweet William, which flower in their second year of growth, often return a third season if cut back immediately after flowering in July.

Perennials with one flush of bloom, such as golden marguerite (*Anthemis tinctorium*) and lily-leafed ladybells (*Adenophora liliifolia*), should be cut back by a third after flowering. By mid- to late August, Shasta daisies and bee balm can be shabby with mildew. I cut them back to the new basal foliage.

Late-summer and autumn-flowering perennials—Late bloomers produce bushy, lower-growing foliage if cut back by half when 4 in. tall, and then by half again when 16 in. tall. You can also stagger flowering by pruning separate plants of the same species a week or so apart.

Pinch chrysanthemums in the spring when plants are 6 in. tall and again when they're 8 in. tall. I pinch at two week intervals until July 15.

TIMETABLE FOR PRUNING HERBACEOUS PLANTS

Prune these plants as necessary throughout the year to shape the plants, promote bloom or remove dead foliage. Cut all of them, except those with winter interest, to the ground in late fall. (Most ornamental grasses are cut to the ground in early spring.)

DEADHEADING

To prolong bloom:

Baby's breath *(Gypsophila paniculata)*, all summer
Blanket flower *(Gaillardia × grandiflora)*, all summer
Bleeding-heart *(Dicentra × 'Luxuriant')*, spring to fall
Bluebell *(Campanula rotundifolia)*, spring to late summer
Daylily *(Hemerocallis)*, summer
Globe amaranth *(Gomphrena globosa)*, summer
Heliopsis *(Heliopsis)*, all summer
Jupiter's-beard *(Centranthus ruber)*, summer
Lanceleaf tickseed *(Coreopsis lanceolata)*, all summer
Larkspur *(Consolida)*, early summer
Lavender *(Lavandula angustifolia)*, summer
Pansy *(Viola × Wittrockiana)*, spring and summer
Phlox *(Phlox maculata, P. paniculata)*, after first bloom
Salvia, summer
Shasta daisy *(Chrysanthemum × superbum)*, all summer
Spring-flowering bulbs *(all)*, old flower stem
Strawflowers *(Helichrysum bracteatum)*, summer
Tussock bellflower *(Campanula carpatica)*, all summer
Veronica *(Veronica spicata)*, all summer
Winged statice *(Limonium sinuatum)*, summer
Yarrow *(Achillea)*, all summer

To prevent seed set:

Amaranthus, summer
Balsam *(Impatiens balsamina)*, summer
Cleome, summer
Columbine *(Aquilegia)*, summer
Phlox *(P. paniculata)*, all summer
Salvia *(Salvia coccinea)*, summer

Daylily flowers last one day, as their name indicates, and then must be deadheaded (above) to focus the plant's energy on the flowers rather than on making seeds. When a flower stem is bloomed-out, the author cuts it close to the ground (left).

Most asters benefit from early season pinching. Pinching promotes compact growth and delayed flowering. Pinching sneezeweed *(Helenium autumnale)* six to eight weeks before it blooms produces bushy, shorter plants. Sedum 'Autumn Joy' will produce more flowers if cut back by half in early summer, when plants are 8 in. tall.

Ornamental grasses—Wait for early spring to cut back most grasses. Let them brighten the winter first: their stems and dry leaves sway in the wind, and their seedheads gleam with frost. Just before new leaves emerge, cut the old leaves and stems back to 6 in. high. Some grasses are better cut back in late summer or fall. I cut back giant reed *(Arundo donax)* in fall, because its stems break down over winter, creating a mess.

Summer heat and drought can dry out grasses, resulting in unsightly brown tips. In late summer I shear or mow ribbon grass *(Phalaris arundinacea* var. *picta)* and variegated bulbous oat grass *(Arrhenatherum elatius* 'Variegatum') to remove scorched foliage.

Ground covers—Mid-summer takes its toll on ground covers as well as flowering perennials. Bishop's weed *(Aegopodium podagraria* 'Variegatum') can brown in mid-summer heat. Simply mow it to the ground to spur regrowth, which will appear in a few weeks. When lamium gets tatty in midsummer, cut it close to the ground—its new growth will last into early winter. Mow creeping lilyturf *(Liriope spicata)* in early spring to remove winter's dead foliage.

Annuals—Pinch most annuals only when you set them out, to encourage branching. But pinch plants grown for their foliage, like coleus, all summer to remove flower buds and to keep the plants full.

Flowering annuals such as cosmos, zinnias, marigolds, petunias, snapdragons, pinks and salvia, need

CUTTING BACK

Alyssum (*Lobularia maritima*), after first bloom, summer

Bee balm (*Monarda didyma*), to ground, late summer

Bishops weed (*Aegopodium podagraria* var. *variegatum*), to ground, midsummer

Candytuft (*Iberis sempervirens*), by half, late spring

Catmint (*Nepeta* × *faassenii, N. mussinii*), by half after first bloom, summer

Creeping lilyturf (*Liriope spicata*), to ground, early spring

Dead nettle (*Lamium maculatum*) 'White Nancy' and 'Beacon Silver',
  to ground, mid-summer

False rock cress (*Aubrieta deltoidea*), by half, late spring

Geranium 'Wargrave Pink' (*Geranium endressii*), to basal foliage, summer

Golden marguerite (*Anthemis tinctoria*), by one-third after blooming, summer

Larkspur (*Delphinium*), to basal foliage, mid-summer

Lavender (*Lavandula angustifolia*), remove dead tips, late spring or early summer

Lilyleaf ladybells (*Adenophora liliifolia*), by one-third after blooming, summer;
  to basal foliage, late summer

Maiden pinks (*Dianthus deltoides*), by half, late spring

Moss phlox (*Phlox subulata*), by half, late spring

Painted daisy (*Chrysanthemum coccineum*), by one-third after blooming, summer

Plumbago (*Ceratostigma plumbaginoides*), to ground, early spring

Russian sage (*Perovskia atriplicifolia*), to ground or live buds, early spring

Sedum 'Autum Joy', by half when 8 in. tall, late spring

Spiderwort (*Tradescantia* × *andersoniana*), by half after first bloom;
  by two-thirds, summer, if needed

Veronica (*Veronica teucrium*), by half, late spring

Yarrow (*Achillea*) Galaxy series, by half, after first bloom; if leggy, summer.
  'Moonshine' and others, old flower stems to basal foliage, late summer

PINCHING

Basil, to prevent flowering, summer

Chrysanthemum (*Chrysanthemum* × *morifolium*), hardy mums, May until early July

Coleus, flower buds, all summer

Michaelmas daisies (*Aster novae-angliae, A. novi-belgii*), early summer until
  early July

Mint (*Mentha*), to prevent flowering, summer

Oregano (*Origanum*), to prevent flowering, summer

Sneezeweed (*Helenium autumnale*), early summer

By early summer, the spring-blooming geranium 'Wargrave Pink' looks unsightly in the author's garden. She prunes the old foliage to the ground, being careful to protect emerging leaves (above). Cutting back reveals a flush of new growth with nicely rounded form and the beginnings of a second bloom period (below).

continuous deadheading during the height of summer to keep them blooming. Cool-season annuals such as pansies may flower through summer's heat if constantly deadheaded.

Certain annuals, notably amaranthus, balsam (*Impatiens balsamina*), calendula, cleome and *Salvia coccinea* are heavy seeders. Deadhead them if you don't want plants everywhere.

Herbs—Lavender should not be pruned until late spring or early summer, after new growth has broken from the old wood. With regular deadheading, it will flower throughout summer.

Disbud basil completely if you're growing it for culinary purposes, because flowering will decrease the flavor of the herb. Disbudding mints and oregano encourages foliage production. Cut mints to the ground in midsummer, and a second crop of tender leaves will develop a few weeks later. Angelica (*Angelica archangelica*) will grow as a perennial if deadheaded; otherwise the plant will self-sow readily.

Fall Cleanup—After several frosts, cut most perennials to the ground and remove the debris. Leave plants with ornamental seed heads or foliage for winter beauty. Don't cut back evergreens like sea pinks (*Armeria maritima*), wild ginger (*Asarum europaeum*) or ferns. Some ferns are evergreen, but even if yours aren't, leave the fronds intact to help protect the crowns from winter injury.

The rewards you reap from deadheading, pinching and cutting back include ornamentals with more flowers and more compact growth and herbs with more flavorful leaves. So grab your pruners, hedge shears, string trimmer or lawn mower, because no matter what the season, you'll find an herbaceous plant in need of timely trimming. □

Tracy DiSabato-Aust is a horticultural consultant, designer and lecturer from Sunbury, Ohio.

Dividing Perennials

One mature plant can yield many new transplants

Many perennials can be divided, as shown here, to start new plants. The clump of soil, roots, and stems at left is a good-sized phlox, dug up gently soon after the new stems emerged from the soil in early spring. The author holds four divisions, just separated from the mother plant. Transplanted and watered regularly, they will soon be thriving plants.

by Nancy Carney

The surest, easiest, most rewarding and least expensive way to increase your supply of perennial plants is division. It's also magical. A single three-year-old plant of phlox can yield five strong, new plants in one growing season. You start in spring with one mother plant and have a thriving family by fall.

Dividing means breaking a plant into pieces that have enough roots and stems to survive and grow on their own after transplanting. Many mature perennial plants could be described as a collection of small, united plants, resulting from stems taking root where they come in contact with soil, or roots producing new stems. To divide a mature plant, you simply dig it up and separate it into suitable pieces.

When I say perennials, I mean herbaceous perennials that die to the ground in the frosts of fall and regrow from the roots in spring. There are dozens of familiar and well-loved examples that can be divided with good prospects for success, including asters, astilbes, coreopsis, chrysanthemums, and phlox. In general, they have fibrous root systems (they have no dominant root, and all roots branch repeatedly), and their stems arise directly from the roots or from a crown, the base of a plant where roots and stems emerge. All of the fibrous-rooted perennials can be divided in much the same way, with allowance for those with tough or brittle roots or woody crowns that must be cut into pieces. Other herbaceous perennials that have deep taproots (milkweed, for example), fleshy underground stems (irises), or bulbs (lilies) are as easy to divide as fibrous-rooted perennials, but require different techniques and timing. In this article, I will talk about dividing fibrous-rooted perennials only.

Techniques for dividing

Perennials differ in their tolerance for division. Some, such as achillea, coreopsis and chrysanthemum, have a mat of slender, shallow roots which makes them easy to divide. You can usually pull the roots apart by hand as easily as you tear a paper napkin. The plants are barely fazed by division—if I'm in a hurry, I will trowel up and transplant a chunk of roots and stems without bothering to first dig up the mother plant.

Another group—including phlox, heliopsis, and helianthus, among others—has slightly deeper roots which knit together in an unyielding tangle as the plants age. Young plants are easy to divide by hand, but older plants require judicious cutting among the roots. Often the roots are brittle and have to be handled with care.

A third group, which includes astilbes and columbines, among others, has similar roots but a crowded and brittle or woody crown. Because roots and stems are bunched tightly together there, you must divide the crown with care, cutting precisely with knife or shears to make pieces with enough stems and roots to take hold and grow.

If you're new to dividing, I recommend you start with the most resilient plants, the kinds our grandmothers grew in country gardens, that thrive in spite of adversity. I've listed 26 widely-grown perennials that are easy to divide in the chart at right.

Dividing in spring

I think early spring is the best time to divide perennials. In many parts of the United States the new plants recover from the shock of division and establish themselves readily, thanks to favorable conditions—moist soil, mild weather and usually dependable rains. In dry climates, spring division works fine, provided you water the new plants regularly. I like to divide a plant when the new growth is just emerging from the ground. Since different perennials awaken at different times, the work spaces itself nicely. Here in Connecticut, in Zone 6, I divide plants over two months, March and April.

Start by lifting a well-established, good-sized plant, roots and all. To do this, spade a circle around the plant, at least 4 in. from the stems, 6 in. if possible. Loosen the soil deeply so you can lift the entire plant without yanking. Once the plant is out of the ground, lay the mass of roots and soil on its side, and tease out most of the soil with your fingers or with a sharp spray from the hose.

Now study the roots and small stems closely, looking for natural divisions—clusters of young stems that stand apart from their neighbors on their own roots. Each cluster can be a new plant, provided it has at least one stem and a substantial mass of roots that you can separate from the other roots more or less intact.

How many divisions you make depends both on the plant and what results you hope to achieve. If you want strong new plants that establish themselves quickly and grow vigorously, divide the mother plant into just a few pieces. On a big plant, you'll lump several natural divisions into each piece. On the other hand, if you don't mind new plants that demand more care to become established and take more time to reach a substantial size, you can split the mother plant into all its natural divisions. I generally divide plants into thirds or quarters because I want big divisions, but when I need a lot of new plants (for example, when I'm starting a new flower bed), I make smaller divisions. I usually allow a new division at least three to five stems, but for very expensive plants, which I want to propagate rapidly over several years, I make more divisions with fewer stems, and baby them. If you are a beginner, it's better to make fewer divisions, which will be more likely to survive because of their larger size.

For plants with thin, shallow roots, you can pull the divisions apart by hand.

Starting at the top of the plant, place one hand on the division you want and the other hand alongside it. Work your fingers into the roots, pulling them apart gently. As roots snap and tear, you may find yourself wondering whether the plant can survive being sundered. It can. If the roots are so snarled that gentle pressure will not separate them, and pulling harder will break too many of them, cut the snarls with a knife or shears. I often treat these plants far more roughly, slicing them into segments with a sharp trowel or spade. I lose more roots, but as long as the divisions are big enough, they recover readily.

When you divide a plant with heavy, matted roots, such as a well-established, mature heliopsis, you have to cut the divisions apart with a knife. Work from the bottom, tracing the roots of your division by eye and then separating them by hand. When you can untangle them no more, begin cutting your way up to the stems. Often a small cut or two will allow you to separate more roots by hand. Continue separating and cutting until your division is free of the mother plant.

For perennials with crowns, you have to be decisive. Often a plant has no obvious natural divisions because its stems are tightly packed together. Look closely at the placement of the roots underneath the crown, and separate the roots into three or four groups. Now look at the top of the crown and decide which stems belong with each group of roots. With a knife or shears, slice through the crown, following a track between the stems and cutting as few roots as possible. Aim for pieces with roughly the same percentage of stems and roots.

Transplanting new divisions

Divisions start life as small, slightly-damaged, bare-root plants, so they need care in handling and transplanting. When you divide a perennial, work quickly and be sure the roots of the mother plant and the divisions never dry out. I promptly slip each new division under a damp cloth, or into a pail of shallow water. On a sunny or windy day, I work in the shade to safeguard the mother plant.

Transplant a new division as you would a small container-grown plant. First, prune away dead or damaged stems and roots. Loosen the soil where you intend to set the new plant, and dig a hole wide enough to spread the roots in. Set the division in the hole at the same depth it was on the mother plant, and carefully work soil around the roots with your fingers. Firm the soil around the division, water it well, and then mulch lightly with compost, shredded leaves, grass clippings or straw.

Regular watering is vital for newly-transplanted divisions. Their root systems

Common easily-divided perennials

Plant	Comments
Yarrow (*Achillea* spp.)	Usually aromatic herbs with flat-topped flower clusters
Everlasting (*Anaphalis* spp.)	Gray or woolly plants. Flowers often cut for drying.
Windflower (*Anemone* spp.)	Good foliage and flowers; some species bloom in fall.
Columbine (*Aquilegia* spp.)	Hardy, branching plants; flowers usually with backward-projecting spur
Wormwood (*Artemisia* spp.)	Usually gray, aromatic herbs; insignificant flowers in spikes; tolerate poor, dry soil.
Aster (*Aster* spp.)	Vigorous plants flower profusely in summer or fall.
Astilbe (*Astilbe* spp.)	Attractive toothed or cut foliage and showy flower stalks; tolerate light shade.
Bellflower (*Campanula* spp.)	Widely varying plants, most with showy flowers.
Chrysanthemums (*Chrysanthemum* spp.)	Familiar fall-blooming plants in many sizes, with daisy-like flowers in many colors.
Coreopsis (*Coreopsis* spp.)	Profusely-flowering plants; most bloom in summer or fall.
Blanket flower (*Gaillardia* spp.)	Flowers usually red or yellow; favorites for cutting.
Cranesbill (*Geranium* spp.)	White, pink or purplish flowers; most plants hardy to Zone 5.
Sunflower (*Helianthus* spp.)	Vigorous, profusely-flowering plants, with showy blooms.
Oxeye (*Heliopsis* spp.)	Summer-blooming sunflower-like plants with yellow or purple ray flowers.
Ligularia (*Ligularia* spp.)	Summer-blooming plants with yellow or orange flowers in clusters.
Lobelia (*Lobelia* spp.)	Vigorous flowering plants, including several natives that tolerate moist soil.
Horsemint (*Monarda* spp.)	Summer-blooming, thistle-shaped flowers
Forget-me-not (*Myosotis* spp.)	Hairy, vigorous plants, with pink, blue or white flowers; tolerate shade and moist soil.
Evening primrose (*Oenothera* spp.)	Widely varying plants, some showy; flowers open by day or in the evening.
Phlox (*Phlox* spp.)	Profusely-flowering plants of many forms; most are hardy.
Cinquefoil (*Potentilla* spp.)	Many species; yellow, white or red flowers; most are hardy.
Primrose (*Primula* spp.)	Low rosette plants with showy flowers on spikes in wide range of colors.
Coneflower (*Rudbeckia* spp.)	Vigorous plants with yellow to reddish-brown flowers in summer and fall.
Goldenrod (*Solidago* spp.)	Vigorous summer- and fall-blooming plants; not to blame for hayfever.
Speedwell (*Veronica* spp.)	Widely-varying plants with flowers in spikes or clusters.

Dividing a perennial

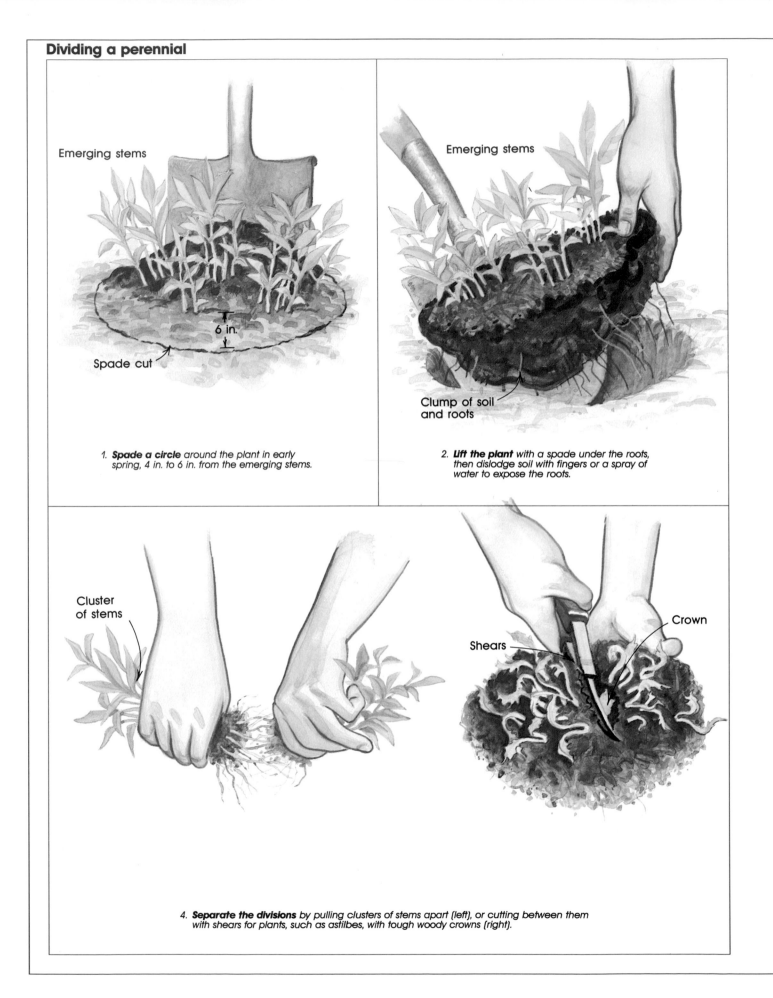

Emerging stems

6 in.

Spade cut

1. **Spade a circle** around the plant in early spring, 4 in. to 6 in. from the emerging stems.

Emerging stems

Clump of soil and roots

2. **Lift the plant** with a spade under the roots, then dislodge soil with fingers or a spray of water to expose the roots.

Cluster of stems

Shears

Crown

4. **Separate the divisions** by pulling clusters of stems apart (left), or cutting between them with shears for plants, such as astilbes, with tough woody crowns (right).

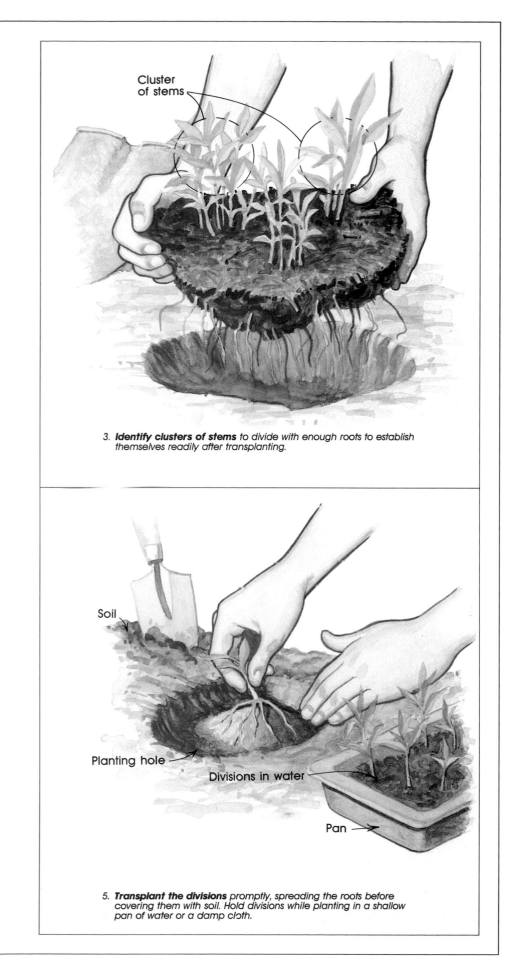

3. **Identify clusters of stems** to divide with enough roots to establish themselves readily after transplanting.

Soil

Planting hole

Divisions in water

Pan

5. **Transplant the divisions** promptly, spreading the roots before covering them with soil. Hold divisions while planting in a shallow pan of water or a damp cloth.

Cluster of stems

will suffer if the top few inches of soil dry out. Treat them as you would plants in small pots. For the first two to four weeks, I water anytime the soil surface dries. For the rest of the season, I water at least once a week whenever rainfall is inadequate.

Dividing in summer and fall

Though I recommend that beginners stick to dividing perennials in spring, with experience you can divide perennials throughout the growing season. I've found that plants in full leaf, and even full flower, can be divided successfully in spite of heat, drought and rough handling, provided I water the new plants diligently until they establish good root systems. After spring, the least risky time for dividing is fall, just as the plants decline or go dormant. Where winters have thaws and freezes, you must safeguard the divisions against frost heaving (soil movement that pushes small plants out of the ground). I mulch fall divisions with 3 in. of leaves and wood chips which nearly eliminates damage from frost heaving.

Though the most risky time to divide perennials is mid-summer, often I divide plants then. When I'm starting a new bed, I can set out divisions in flower and see color from the start.

For summer division, I try to pick an overcast day, with a threat of rain in the forecast. I work in the late afternoon to spare the newly-transplanted divisions from sunlight as long as possible. I do not cut back the leaves or flowers, but I usually stake the divisions. They're top heavy, and wind, rain or an animal can easily tip them over and expose the roots, which would dry out and die in a few hours.

If you divide perennials anytime between late spring and early fall, take special care that the new plants have adequate moisture. I mulch right after transplanting. If the next few days are sunny, I'll cover the divisions with boxes or cloth. I mist big divisions that are in flower every few hours during the day, and I water all divisions, big or small, once or twice daily for the first two weeks. In hot sunny weather, the plants often partially die back, losing some of their leaves, but I've never lost a division.

I hope dividing perennials does not strike you as a great deal of work. Just choose a perennial and start. Once you've grown healthy new plants which cost you only a few pleasant minutes playing with dirt and roots and a few hours of watering, you will want to make dividing perennials a constant part of your gardening. You can divide the plants you have to fill out your garden, and spend the money you save on the plants of your dreams. ☐

Nancy Carney's garden in Newtown, Connecticut, multiplies by division.

Dividing Suckering Shrubs

Quick propagation with a shovel and shears

by Nancy Carney

I have moved several times to homes that were new only to me and in need of landscaping. My budget never allowed for buying much nursery stock, yet I always wanted a planted place immediately. Over the years, I learned to fill in a new property by dividing suckering shrubs—species that send up new stems each year from the crown and roots, forming clumps that can be dug up and split into as many pieces as there are stems with roots. Usually my new homes came with suitable shrubs, which I divided repeatedly. I've also bought common and inexpensive species from nurseries, and, reverting to a childhood practice, dug others from woods and overgrown fields and divided them, too. To date I've divided more than 50 species. I pared that list to some favorites in the chart on pp. 74-75.

If your house is more than 20 years old and has had an owner or two, you're likely to find some of these shrubs on the property. They may be out of fashion, too close together and poorly located, but consider their merits. Their owners probably did not water, fertilize, mulch or spray the plants, yet they survived. They are also free. Once you know that these large specimens can probably be divided into five to 20 new plants, it's obvious what to do with them. In a word, recycle.

We purchased our current home, a Connecticut farmhouse with three acres, seven years ago. Most of the land was devoted to a riding ring and paddock for horses. It was a botanical wasteland, except for some fine trees and the foundation plantings of kerria, lilac, yew, mock orange and forsythia that reached the second story of the house, causing wood rot and gloom.

I began dividing the foundation shrubs before I unpacked. I also bought 2-gal. pots of trusty species such as clethra, hydrangea, shrub roses, *Abeliophyllum distichum* (which I call white for-

Nancy Carney adds shrubs to her property by dividing specimens that she finds on her land or in the wild, or buys in containers. Here she carries a kerria (*Kerria japonica*) that she uprooted alongside her house to make divisions for a hedgerow.

Carney started this hedge of clethra (*Clethra alnifolia*) five years ago with six divisions taken from one nursery plant in a 2-gal. pot.

sythia) and potentilla, and I collected maple-leaved raspberry, hobblebush, mountain laurel and multiflora rose from the wild and divided all of them. Within five years, the property was a planted place. My inherited forsythia became a 300-ft.-long row, the multiflora rose became a fragrant and impenetrable 400-ft.-long hedge, and I had divided the potentilla so extensively that I began to think of it as invasive.

The first rule of division is that each piece, whether it comprises one or several stems, must have adequate roots. Frankly, you learn what is adequate through experience. Some suckering shrubs are much more tolerant of misjudgment than others are; a few, such as pussy willow, forsythia and clethra, strike root so readily, especially in early spring, that their divisions need fewer roots than do those of other plants. For the newcomer to dividing shrubs, I particularly suggest forsythia, kerria, spirea and lilac. They accept division readily, and they are valuable ornamentals. (If you must buy them, you'll find that they're also among the most common and inexpensive nursery shrubs.) For all suckering shrubs, however, I think that much less root is needed than is commonly believed, if the gardener is willing to take proper care of the transplants.

The number of divisions a shrub can yield is determined by how many stems bear roots. You can't be sure until you expose the crown of the plant. For photo-

graphs to accompany this article, I had intended to use a shrub rose from the garden that I thought would yield three to eight divisions. But when I dug down about 6 in., I found that all the stems were branches—not one had independent roots. In contrast, my original forsythia clump, which had at least 500 stems, yielded about 300 divisions. Smaller shrubs and potted nursery plants yield fewer divisions. When I buy nursery plants, I pay more attention to the number of stems than to the show of flowers. I also check the condition of the stems. If some are young, still soft and green, or even tiny knobs just emerging from the soil, the plant is thriving, in spite of its cramped living quarters, and is likely to offer good divisions. On plants of any size, I look for stems with prominent buds and shoots at their base (see photo, p. 74). These will produce new stems, rapidly filling in a new division.

Though many authorities recommend cutting back the top of a division to balance the roots lost during digging and dividing, I rarely cut back any of the shrubs listed in the chart unless they're taller than 8 ft. I don't want to lose any top growth—I want the plant to fill out and look mature rapidly. In the last few years, I've trimmed some divisions to 8 ft., but only so I can lug and plant them more easily. I've moved 15-ft.-tall lilacs on a number of occasions and not taken a foot off their height. Occasionally, when the weather is hot and dry and I can't water, I cut back divisions by one-third, but if I can water, I

don't cut back at all, and the divisions soon establish themselves.

When should you divide shrubs? I ignore the usual guidelines about dividing during dormancy. I don't think the shrub exists that can't be divided in the middle of July, provided it's cosseted, mainly by regular watering, for the rest of the season. I like to fix a misting hose or a spray nozzle above the plants and keep the water on throughout the daylight hours during the first two weeks. Keeping the leaves watered lets them nourish new root growth. If I can't rig an overhead spray (because of the distance from a well), I'm willing to carry water by the bucket and use a sprinkling can on the plants four or five times a day for at least two weeks, and then once a day for the remainder of the summer. I made hundreds of divisions when we moved here in July. My outdoor well went dry in August, and I carried buckets of water from the house for hours every day. I didn't lose a single division.

If you prefer less intensive maintenance, divide your shrubs during dormancy. For most gardeners, that means working in the late spring or early fall. From Zone 4 northward, I suggest dividing only in the spring, so that the new plants have the whole season to establish roots and recover before they have to suffer the rigors of winter. From Zone 5 south, you can divide during the winter whenever the ground is diggable. Here on the northern edge of Zone 6, I divide until

Carney divides nursery plants before setting them in the garden. She buys multi-stemmed potted specimens, like this hybrid azalea from a 2-gal. pot (above left). By pulling gently on the stems, she broke the roots apart and made two divisions (above right).

Christmas, and then I start again when favorable weather returns, occasionally as early as February. Sometimes the top few inches of the ground is still frozen, but once I dig through, I find friable soil. I water dormant divisions far less than I do those with leaves. If the weather is warm, I give the roots water once a day for a week. If a good rain falls, I skip watering.

Whenever you divide, you should minimize stress on the plants. When I can, I work in the rain, or on a cloudy day just before a rain. Otherwise, I divide shrubs in the early evening so that the new plants have some time in the ground without sun. I have a bucket of water on hand and put the divisions in it as I make them. During dry weather, I let the roots soak for several hours. When I plant divisions during the winter, I make sure that there are no air pockets around the roots. I place the divisions in the planting hole or trench, backfill half the soil, water twice and work the soil with my fingers, and then add the remaining backfill.

I divided the six-year-old kerria in the photos at the beginning of July during a drought. The kerria started out five years ago as a single stem with a fist-sized ball of roots, grew into a 6-ft.-tall shrub with four dozen stems, and threatened to compete with nearby lilies-of-the-valley and azaleas. I spaded a 2-ft. circle around the plant to cut the roots and lifted the clump from the ground. You need only 6 in. to 8 in. of roots around the clump for good divisions. After removing the clump, I kept an eye on the site and pulled out any suckers that arose from the roots left in the ground.

To make good divisions, you need a clear look at the roots and crown of a shrub. In this case, the soil was so dry that I could shake it off the roots. If the soil adheres, use a sharp spray from a garden hose to dislodge the dirt. Once you've removed the dirt, gently pull the stems apart. Where the crown refuses to split on its own, or where you run into a ganglion of roots, separate the stems with a pair of pruning shears. This is the step that scares most people, and they separate their plant into fewer pieces than they could. Don't be afraid to hack away. Remember, all you need is a stem with a few roots. I made 20 divisions of the kerria, most of them multi-stemmed, for a 20-ft.-long hedgerow in front of a fence. I could have made twice as many divisions if I had needed them.

I plant divisions in individual holes or in trenches. For the kerria, I dug a trench along the fence. I couldn't dig deeper than 4 in. because the soil there is thick with the shallow roots of swamp maples. I set the divisions in the trench and curled the roots to fit the shallow depression. Most books say that curled roots eventually

EASILY DIVIDED SHRUBS

Name	Height (ft.)	Hardiness zone	Comments
Abeliophyllum distichum	5	5	Fragrant white flowers in early Apr., two weeks before forsythia.
Calycanthus floridus Carolina allspice, sweet shrub	8	4	Fragrant, reddish-brown, 2-in. flowers in May; a native favored by the Colonials.
Caryopteris × clandonensis Blue mist shrub	3	5	Intense blue and purple flower spikes from Aug. to frost; favored by bees; dies to the ground in winter with no ill effect in the N.E.
Clethra alnifolia Summer-sweet, sweet pepperbush	8	3	Highly fragrant white and pink flower spikes from Aug. to frost; favored by bees.
Deutzia gracilis	3	5	White or pink flower clusters in June; graceful shrub.
Forsythia × intermedia Golden-bells	4-12	4	Yellow wands of flowers in Apr. before leaves; good for hedges; stems root readily in moist spring soil.
Hydrangea spp. H. *arborescens* H. *paniculata* 'Tardiva'	6 10	4 5	Large white flower clusters.
Ilex verticillata Winterberry	12	3	Unbelievable scarlet pea-sized berries hold most of the winter; electrifying color.
Kerria japonica Japanese rose	4-6	4	Single or double yellow flowers in May and showy green branches all winter.
Kolkwitzia amabilis Beautybush	10	4	Profuse true pink trumpets in May; graceful arching form.
Lonicera fragrantissima Winter honeysuckle	6	5	Highly fragrant, tiny white flowers in Mar.; delicate, graceful arching form.
Philadelphus spp. Mock orange P. *coronarius* P. × *virginalis*	2-12	Some to 3	Single and double white flowers in May; up to 2½ in.; some are highly fragrant; hundreds of hybrids.

Near the base of this large kerria stem are several vigorous suckers and prominent buds, which will develop into new stems. This division will speedily make a full-looking shrub.

Name	Height (ft.)	Hardiness zone	Comments
Potentilla fruticosa Shrubby cinquefoil	3	3	Single flowers from May to Oct.; white, pink, yellow and red shades; delicate and airy foliage.
Rhododendron spp. Azaleas	3-10	4-5	Many species and hybrids with different bloom periods and colors; must never dry out, so mulch new plants well and water frequently.
Ribes odoratum Clove currant	6	4	Fragrant yellow flowers in May.
Rosa spp.			
R. Hugonis	7	3	Small, single yellow flowers in May; graceful.
R. multiflora	12	4	Highly fragrant clusters of small white/pink flowers in May; good for hedges.
R. rugosa	6	3	Large purple-red, pink and white flowers in June and sporadically; grows anywhere.
Rubus odoratus Maple-leaved raspberry	6	3	Blooms from June to Sept.; fragrant, 2-in. purple-red single flowers followed by sour raspberry fruits; huge maple-shaped leaves.
Salix discolor Pussy willow	20	3	Catkins from Feb. to Mar.; branches root if stuck in moist spring soil.
Spiraea spp. Bridal-wreath	5-9	5	Flat white flower clusters in May; delicate foliage and arching growth; many different types.
S. prunifolia			
S. × Vanhouttei			
Syringa spp. Lilac			Highly fragrant, white to lavender flower clusters in May; indispensable for fragrance; can be cut to ground and will regrow; good for hedges.
S. Meyeri	6	5	
S. microphylla	6	5	
S. patula	6	5	
S. × persica	6	5	
S. vulgaris	20	3	
Viburnum alnifolium Hobblebush	10	3	Flat, large white flower clusters in Apr.; huge seersucker leaves; other viburnums can be divided, but I haven't tried them.

After cleaning away the dirt to expose the crown and roots, Carney breaks the kerria apart by hand, and then makes smaller divisions by separating the roots and stems with shears. If she needs many divisions, she uses single stems, like the two shown at the bottom of the photo, which have roots that are more than adequate.

strangle themselves. While I believe this for trees and many shrubs, I find that the roots of suckering shrubs accept cramped quarters, probably because the plant sends new suckers and roots out in every direction so rapidly. On this property, I rarely amend the soil when I plant. If the soil is poor, I add compost. Kerria is tough, and the soil along the fence was good, so I simply dug the trench for the divisions. If I had divided a more delicate shrub, I would have brought in good soil and tried to dig deeper.

To support the kerria divisions, I tied a branch from each division to a nail set in the fence. I used No. 6 galvanized siding nails, which don't rust, and tapped them lightly into the fence so that I can remove them this year. For small divisions, I've used thumbtacks and carpet tacks. In the open, I tie most divisions to thin stakes. I tie lilacs, which are heavier, to 2-in. by 2-in. posts.

I spread a 2-in.-thick layer of mulch around the kerria divisions. I didn't have any leaves, my usual mulch, so I used excelsior saved from a shipment of daylilies, and semi decomposed bark from my woodpile. For divisions, I don't think that the kind of mulch matters, as long as it shades the roots and prevents evaporation.

I watered the new plants four times a day for two weeks. I couldn't spray their leaves after that (I was away on a trip), and unfortunately it didn't rain for several weeks. Though the swamp maples partially shaded the divisions, eventually the stems lost the top third of their leaves, which was an excessive amount, much greater than any dieback I had seen the July I moved here.

Even if new divisions drop all their leaves, don't despair. One July, 15 years ago, I hacked lilacs out of an abandoned field, carried them with their roots exposed to the moving air in the back of a station wagon to a site 30 miles away, and divided them. Every leaf fell off the divisions within the first week, but then new leaves appeared. The plants became a dense hedge within a few years. I no longer own that property, but the hedge survives.

The division of suckering shrubs is not only an inexpensive and speedy way to acquire plants, but also gives me the pleasure of propagation. I can start a border from a favorite plant that is no longer sold in the nursery trade, or divide it into treasured gifts for gardening friends, who may hack away at their clump in a few years and pass the rarity on to new gardeners. If everyone concerned makes divisions with adequate roots and waters diligently, recycling shrubs can go on forever. □

Nancy Carney lives in Newtown, Conn.

Moving a Small Shrub
Tips for first-time transplanters

With attention to a few rules of thumb, and help from her friend Ann, author Eddison successfully moved a long-suffering oakleaf hydrangea to a more hospitable site. First, they dug a trench around the plant to make a root ball the same diameter as the leaf canopy (top left). After digging down and under the plant, they heaved it onto a tarp with as little disturbance to the root ball as possible (above). Twisting the tarp to form a sling, they moved the plant to its new home (top right). Only minutes after being dug out, the hydrangea was in place in its new home. Ann added soil up to the previous soil line after giving the transplant a good soaking in the new hole (left). Two years after transplanting, Eddison's oakleaf hydrangea flourishes in the dry shade of an old maple (right). The green-leaved hosta 'Royal Standard' makes a fine companion.

by Sydney Eddison

Gardeners are forever moving plants from one spot in the garden to another. The combination you thought would be so pleasing isn't, the plant that seemed ideal for the conditions wasn't. If you haven't done it before, moving a small shrub might seem a daunting task. The plant is likely to be bigger than most of the herbaceous perennials you've ever transplanted, and probably cost a lot more. But moving a small shrub needn't be traumatic—for you or the shrub. Over the years, I've relocated many small (and not so small) shrubs and found that following a few simple rules makes the job manageable and the shrub happy. I've even bent a few of the rules and gotten away with it.

About five years ago, I planted an oakleaf hydrangea on a parched slope beneath a large maple tree. Dry shade is

impossible for many plants, but I had hopes for the hydrangea (see the sidebar on the facing page). For two years the plant tolerated the conditions; it even bloomed. But it didn't thrive and it hardly grew at all. I decided to rescue it.

The best time to transplant a deciduous shrub is when the plant is fully dormant—in the fall after it's lost its leaves or in the spring before new ones appear. I much prefer early spring in our area, so the plant can have a full season in its new site before winter. A recently moved specimen requires additional moisture. If a plant is moved in the fall and the ground freezes prematurely, the roots can't take up water.

Unfortunately, by the time my friend Ann was able to help me with the move—the root ball of even a small shrub is heavy—the hydrangea was in leaf. As the plant could only decline in vigor left where it was, I decided to go ahead and move it—leaves or no leaves. We talked about cutting it back before the move to conserve moisture. But in the end, we figured least done soonest mend-

ed. (A leafier plant than mine would lose much more water through transpiration and would be a better candidate for pruning.) The soil around the plant was still moist from earlier rains, otherwise I would have given it a good soaking a day or two beforehand. Damp earth clings to roots much better than dry earth does.

If the timing of our undertaking wasn't perfect, there were other circumstances that improved our chances of success. We were moving the hydrangea to a bed that was ready and waiting. In the shade of yet another maple, the new bed was raised about a foot above the surrounding soil by an informal retaining wall of large boulders. For the previous four years, I'd been putting down layers of mulch hay in the bed, and it had finally decomposed to a velvety compost. Ann and I mixed this with the topsoil beneath, adding peat moss and stirring it all together. The result was so soft and rich that you could push your arm into it up to your elbow. Even the most tentative new feeder roots would have no difficulty

Photos: bottom right, Sydney Eddison; all others, Staff

reaching out, and the water-retentive peat moss would go a long way toward counteracting the drying effect of the maple roots.

In the best of all possible worlds, I would move a shrub in the late afternoon so it would have reduced light and the cool of the evening in which to recuperate a little. Heat, sun and wind steal moisture that's critical to recovery. Ann could come only in the early morning, however, which is the next best time for transplanting.

First, we dug a trench around the hydrangea. In order to move the plant with as little disturbance as possible to the feeder roots and to conserve the maximum amount of moisture, I wanted a big mass of earth around the roots. A root ball the same diameter as the spread of the plant's leafy canopy should be enough. The hydrangea's canopy and therefore the inside diameter of our trench was about 30 in. When we'd dug the trench to the full depth of the shovel, we felt around under the plant for any big, deep roots, which would have to be severed. Luckily, there weren't any. Then, from opposite sides of the trench, we dug deeper and toward the center of the plant. Upon meeting, we got down on our knees, worked our arms under the root ball and hauled the hydrangea out of the ground, easing it onto a waiting tarpaulin.

We made a sling by twisting the ends of the tarp, and gently carried the shrub between us to its new site. There we eased it into a waiting hole, a bit larger in diameter but the same depth as the root ball. Ann then began backfilling with the compost-rich soil, firming it around the roots as she went along. When about half the soil had been returned to the hole, she soaked the plant until water pooled in the hole. After the water had been absorbed, she filled the remainder of the hole, bringing the fill up to the line on the trunk indicating the level of the soil at the previous site, and tamping the soil by hand and, finally, by foot. She then formed a soil moat around the shrub to catch rainwater, gave the plant a final soaking, and dressed the whole bed with 4 in. of shredded leaves to conserve moisture. As the hydrangea was already in leaf, we were worried about the leaves wilting in the sun—it was too early in the season for the maple to provide shade. We rigged up a circle of stakes around the shrub and draped a sheet over them like a tent.

We left the sheet in place until the maple leaves provided enough shade. That summer, I kept a close eye on the hydrangea, but it never looked back. It grew more in that year than in the two previous years. By the end of the next season, it had almost doubled in size. □

Sydney Eddison gardens in Newtown, CT.

Shrub for a dry, shady spot

As a confirmed—or perhaps I should say chronic—impulse buyer, I frequently forget just how and why a plant found its way into my garden. But this is not the case with the oakleaf hydrangea (*Hydrangea quercifolia*). I remember exactly when I got it and why. In the fall of 1984, I went to a lecture at the New York Botanical Garden given by Pamela Harper, a gardener, writer and speaker whom I admire for her knowledge and for the wonderful plant combinations she arranges in her own Virginia garden. Her lecture was entitled "Easy Plants for Difficult Situations." One of the problem situations she addressed was dry shade.

We have 11 mature maple trees within the confines of our garden, which means 11 large areas of dry shade. Maples, in addition to being shallow-rooted—which means that they rob a wide area of the surrounding soil of moisture and nutrients—also have masses of overlapping leaves that create deep shadow and keep out rain. According to Ms. Harper and my own experience, no plant actually "prefers" dry shade, but some tolerate it quite cheerfully. Oakleaf hydrangea is one such long-suffering plant. The slide she showed by way of illustration was of a large, mounded shrub with rich green foliage and masses of white flower heads shaped like the blossoms of garden phlox, only much larger and slightly elongated. At the base of this handsome plant was a solid planting of the blue-leaved hosta 'Halcyon'. I was very struck by the mutually complementary association. As hostas had done well under many of my maples, I thought I would try a similar planting.

The next spring, I ordered the shrub and it duly arrived—bare-rooted, dormant and not prepossessing to look at, but otherwise in full health and strength. It was about 18 in. to 24 in. tall, and had three main woody shoots and a few side twigs. I potted it up and put it under the lath house until it began to put out leaves. I often keep young shrubs in pots for several weeks. It's easier to keep a daily eye on them to see if they need water. The shade of the lath roof protects them from too much sun, and they're out of the drying wind there. In early summer, I planted the hydrangea in the garden and surrounded it with hostas.

The site was one of the most problematic on the whole property—on top of quite a steep slope among large rocks at the foot of one of the maples. It was the acid test for any plant. Although I prepared the planting area with plenty of peat moss and compost, the surrounding soil was powdery and bone-dry, and rain tends to run off the slope. During dry spells I watered, but the plants did not thrive. The hosta leaves turned brown around the edges. The hydrangea actually bloomed, but it barely grew at all in two years, which is why I decided to move it.

The plant flourishes in its new bed. The bushy foliage is laden with flowers for four weeks each July, and it's not far from reaching its mature height of 5 ft. to 6 ft. What made the difference? The new site is very shady, receiving only three or four hours of sun a day. It's dry and I don't water, but the heavily amended soil holds water well (we get 40 in. or so of precipitation a year) and is much more fertile.

I've read that oakleaf hydrangea, which grows wild from Georgia to Florida and west to the Mississippi, may die down to the ground during a northern winter and not bloom the following year, but that hasn't happened to mine—yet. Even if it does, I'd still grow it for its good-looking foliage, which in the fall turns a deep mahogany-purple and persists well into November.   —S.E.

Grafting Basics
Advice and methods for first-time success

Tree roses (left) and the dwarf potted peach (above) are two examples of grafted plants. Most tree roses are created by grafting an interstock, which forms the tall, straight stem, onto a rootstock. A year later, the desired rose cultivar is budded at the top of the interstock. 'Garden Gold' peach was budded onto 'Nemaguard', a peach rootstock that's resistant to nematodes.

by Malcolm M. Manners

Among the skills I teach as a college instructor of horticulture is how to graft woody ornamental plants and fruit-tree species. I find that a lot of people are fascinated by the idea of grafting plants, and many have attempted a few grafts in their own gardens. Usually such attempts result in failure, leading to the idea that grafting is a difficult process that most people simply can't learn. But that's just not the case. In fact, I've found that nearly anyone can become a proficient grafter, once the common reasons for failure are understood.

Grafting is a process in which a part of one plant (for example, a piece of stem or a bud) is surgically attached to a part of another plant (a root or a stem with roots). These parts grow together to form a single plant. The part that will eventually grow to form the top of the plant, pro-

ducing stems, leaves, flowers and fruit, is called the scion (pronounced sigh-on). Stems from which scions are cut are called budsticks or budwood. The bottom portion of the graft, which will produce the root system, is known as the rootstock, understock or simply stock. The point at which the scion and rootstock are joined and heal together is the graft union or union. Budding is merely a type of grafting in which the scion is quite small, consisting of just one axillary bud (from the point on a stem just above where a leaf was attached) and a small shield of bark.

The mere fact that a plant is grafted doesn't make it better than a non-grafted plant. Rather, it's the fact that a superior, selected scion is attached to a root system ideally suited to certain growing conditions. The right combination is what makes the grafted plant superior.

Good reasons to graft

Grafting requires more skilled labor and considerably more effort than does growing plants from seeds or rooted cuttings, so grafted plants are generally more

expensive than those produced by other means. Still, there are good reasons to graft some plants.

Grafted plants are usually more uniform in growth habit, flower color, flowering season, and fruit size, shape and quality than are seed-grown plants. If you plant seeds from a 'Golden Delicious' apple, none of the resulting trees would produce typical 'Golden Delicious' fruit. But grafted trees, using scions cut from a 'Golden Delicious' tree, would *all* produce the characteristic apples.

Grafted plants often begin to flower or to bear fruit much sooner than do plants grown from seeds. The scion, cut from a mature tree, continues to behave as a mature stem, flowering and fruiting in spite of the fact that it's now part of a small, grafted plant. Seedlings of most woody plant species have a juvenile period, during which they're unable to flower or bear fruit. (There are a few exceptions to this—'Northern Spy' apples, 'Stuart' pecans and cultivars of *Magnolia campbellii* revert to juvenility at grafting.) Many nursery-grown ornamental species are seedlings. In the East, the southern magnolia (*Magnolia grandiflora*) is nearly always sold as a seedling tree. Gardeners wait five to ten years for such trees to flower, whereas grafted trees normally flower the following year. Most apple trees behave in a similar manner—seedling trees may take many years to begin to bear fruit, but grafted trees will bear when quite young. Trees purchased from a nursery are almost always grafted, but if you have a volunteer fruit-tree seedling in your garden, you can take advantage of its established root system by grafting a cultivated variety onto it.

Grafting a plant allows you to select a root system adapted to your climate and soil, or one that's resistant to local pests and diseases. Some rootstocks produce extreme vigor in the scion; others cause the scion to be dwarfed.

Finally, a skilled grafter can propagate more species, often with better success, than could be accomplished by rooting cuttings or air-layering.

Most fruit- and nut-tree species are commonly grafted, including apples, pears, peaches, plums, cherries, citrus, some grapes, walnuts, pecans and avocados. Woody ornamental plants that are commonly grafted include blue spruce, some magnolias, most roses, gardenias, camellias and tree peonies.

Grafts are usually most successful between members of the same species. Some plants can be grafted onto other species in the same genus—for example, oranges on lemon roots (both genus *Citrus*) or peaches on plum roots (both genus *Prunus*)—or, much less commonly, to another genus in the same family, such as orange on trifoliate orange roots (genus *Poncirus* but still in the citrus family, Rutaceae). Grafts between different plant families generally don't form a union at all, and in any case never survive long enough to make a desirable plant.

Tips for successful grafting

Use a sharp knife. A grafting knife needs to be literally razor-sharp. I test my knife by shaving hair from my arm. If the hair won't shave cleanly, the knife isn't sharp enough. (Don't test a properly sharpened grafting knife with your thumb, or you may need stitches.) A dull knife almost guarantees failure. Our knives are sharpened professionally at a local shop, and I frequently touch up the edge during grafting with a leather razor strop. You can use nearly any style of knife, but I recommend one designed specifically for grafting—these are beveled and honed on only one side, leaving the other side flat. With such a blade, it's easier to make a smooth cut in a woody stem.

To sharpen a grafting knife, use a fine whetstone, such as a hard Arkansas. Lubricate the surface with several drops of

How to treat dormant-grafted, deciduous fruit trees

If you're grafting deciduous fruit trees such as apples, using dormant budwood and rootstocks, the newly grafted trees need some special treatment before being planted in the garden. Bundle the finished grafts in damp newspaper wrapped firmly around the roots. Place the bundle in an opaque plastic bag and tie it firmly shut above the newspaper so that no moisture wicks out. Keep the bag at room temperature to quicken the forming of the callus tissue. Every few days, open the bag and check the newspaper for moisture. After three weeks, buds should be opening. Plant the little trees outdoors in a sheltered spot. Throughout the growing season, rub off any buds that break on the rootstock to give the full thrust of the plant's energy to the scion. —*Ruth Haskell*

oil and hold the blade at a slight angle—say, 10°—beveled side down, against the stone. Move the blade in a circular motion, pressing it lightly against the stone. When you have a good edge, turn the knife over (flat side against the stone), and *very lightly* draw it away from the sharpened edge. Finish by stropping on alternate sides, pulling the knife along the leather away from the sharpened edge.

Cut scions from fresh, healthy budwood. Collect budsticks from young, firm stems. I like to use stems that are no longer succulent, and have produced some wood. Rose stems are at an ideal stage when the flowers are fading and dropping petals. For many fruit trees, the most recent growth flush can be used after it has hardened. Some recalcitrant species, such as mangoes, graft best if the wood is cut just as buds begin to swell for a new growth flush. (If you have problems grafting a particular plant, try again when the buds begin to swell.)

Immediately remove all leaves to prevent wilting. Wilted budwood usually won't make a successful graft union. Place the wood in a plastic bag with a few drops of water, a damp paper towel or a bit of moist peat moss, and seal the bag. In a shady, cool spot, the wood should last several days; if left in the sun, it may die within minutes. Budsticks of many species can survive several months in the refrigerator, if they're kept moist.

Use vigorous rootstocks. Rootstock plants can be seed-grown, or, in some cases, rooted from cuttings. Keep them well watered for several weeks before and after grafting. Wilted rootstocks often result in failed grafts.

Cut cleanly and with confidence. When cutting, use the entire knife blade, starting with the base of the blade and moving out to the tip in a single, sweeping cut. This results in a smoother cut than you would get by whittling, sawing, or pulling a single spot on the knife blade through the entire cut. Splinters, bumps or other imperfections in the cuts may prevent a good match of scion to stock, reducing your success rate.

It's important to complete a graft as quickly as possible. Unprotected cut surfaces may dry out in seconds, preventing a good union from forming. I like to wrap a graft within five to ten seconds of the time I start to cut the wood. Beginning grafters find it difficult to make perfect cuts quickly. The only remedy for this problem is practice.

Practice pays off. I normally use the long canes of a climbing rose variety when teaching beginning grafters. The students cut scions from the canes and reattach them elsewhere on the same cane, pretending that it's a rootstock stem. They can make 10 to 20 practice grafts on a long stem. When they've become adept,

Veneer grafting

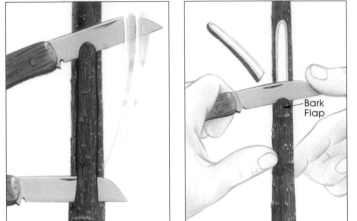

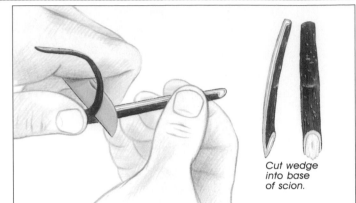

Cut wedge into base of scion.

Rootstock cuts—Slice a thin layer (veneer) of bark away from the stem, about 3 in. to 4 in. long. Cut deep enough to expose the wood, but not deeply into the wood. Start cutting with the base of the knife blade and end at the tip, making the entire cut in a single motion. This will help you achieve a smoother surface, without jagged edges or bumps. In this sequence, star fruit is being grafted. Remove the bark piece from the first cut, leaving a ½-in. flap at the base. The flap will hold the scion in place until you wrap it.

Scion cuts—Use a scion stick about 3 in. long, with at least one bud on it, and preferably several. Remove a thin layer of bark from what will be the back side of the scion. Don't cut half the scion away—you should remove only the bark and perhaps a very thin sliver of wood. To avoid being cut, keep your thumb relaxed as you draw the knife so that as the knife moves, your thumb rides ahead of it. Remove a piece of wood from the bottom of the scion, entering from the front side with your knife, to make the base of the scion into a sharp wedge, which will fit under the flap on the rootstock cut. Be sure the scion is right side up; grafts with an upside-down scion usually don't grow well.

Chip budding

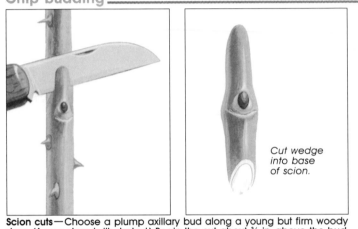

Cut wedge into base of scion.

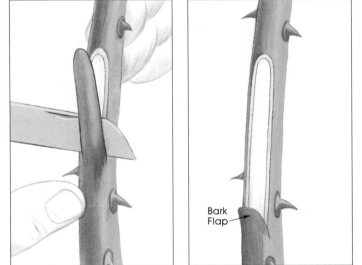

Bark Flap

Scion cuts—Choose a plump axillary bud along a young but firm woody stem. (A rose stem is illustrated.) Begin the cut about ¾ in. above the bud. Starting at the base of your knife blade and ending at the tip, make a single slicing cut behind the bud, to about ¾ in. below the bud. Cut deep enough to enter the wood only slightly, perhaps one-fifth to one-quarter the total thickness of the stem. As is done in veneer grafting, cut a sharp wedge in the bottom of the scion, to fit into the flap at the base of the rootstock cut. Having the wedge at the bottom also decreases the chances of attaching the scion upside-down. The finished scion will be 1 in. to 1½ in. long. Scions that are too short reduce the chances for success.

Rootstock cuts—Cut away a piece of bark similar in size and shape to the scion chip. Cut a bark flap at the base to hold the scion during wrapping. As with the scion chip, don't cut deeply into the stem—one-fifth of its total thickness is about right.

---

they throw away the practice wood and move on to a real scion and rootstock. No precious rootstock plants or scions have been wasted, and they're remarkably better grafters than they were 15 minutes earlier. If you try this method, practice on the species you intend to graft. If you're budding roses, don't practice on apple wood, which has an entirely different feel under the knife.

Keep the wood moist and clean. In addition to working quickly, you can prevent the cut surfaces of your scion from drying by making those cuts first, then storing the scion cut-side-down on your tongue while you work on the rootstock. Of course, scions of toxic species or plants you've recently sprayed with an pesticide

shouldn't be placed in your mouth, but most commonly-grafted plants are harmless. I use this trick with roses, citrus and magnolias (which taste bad). Commercial citrus budders often cut large numbers of scion buds at once, storing them in their cheeks for later use. Saliva is harmless to the buds and doesn't seem to promote rotting or other problems.

Cut surfaces should not come in contact with the soil, which contains bacteria and fungi. Unless scions are in scarce supply, discard any that are dropped.

Tape grafts firmly. I wrap grafts with ½-in. clear polyethylene budding tape (not gummed). The wrap should be quite firm, stretching the tape almost to the point of breaking. Plastic tape must be tied

securely at the end. Another wrapping material that has gained popularity in recent years is Parafilm, a very stretchy, waxy material originally developed for sealing laboratory glassware. It has the advantage of not having to be unwrapped later, as does tape, since the growing scion eventually stretches and splits the Parafilm. Also, if stretched correctly, Parafilm sticks to itself, making it unnecessary to tie off the end of the wrap. Trim Parafilm to a convenient width before wrapping.

In warm weather, I normally leave a graft wrapped three to six weeks, depending on the species. When callus tissue has developed on all the cut surfaces, the graft is probably ready to be unwrapped. (Callus is the wound-healing

Illustrations: Pat Schories

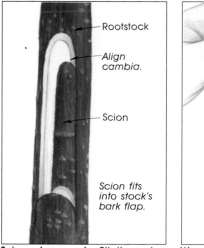

- Rootstock
- *Align cambia.*
- Scion
- *Scion fits into stock's bark flap.*

Cut notch.

Remove rootstock top.

Scion placement—Fit the scion into the stock's bark flap. If the scion is narrower than the stock, align the scion along one side of the rootstock cut. The cambia of the scion and the stock must be aligned.

Wrap the graft—Wrap tightly from bottom to top, keeping the two cambia properly aligned. Tie off grafting tape with a half-hitch knot. If using Parafilm, stretch and press the end against the previous turn.

Aftercare—After several weeks, carefully unwrap the graft and cut a deep notch into the rootstock bark just above the scion. This will encourage the scion to begin growth. Once it has produced a strong, leafy stem, you can completely remove the rootstock top, leaving only the scion to form the top of the plant. Stake the scion to make it grow straight and upright, and to prevent its being broken off by the wind.

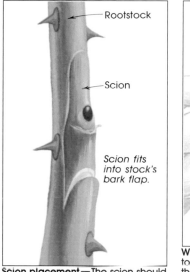

- Rootstock
- Scion
- *Scion fits into stock's bark flap.*

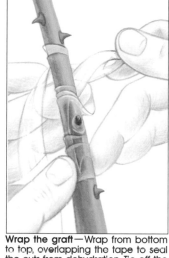

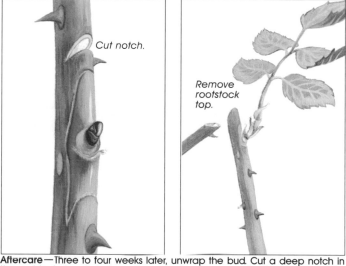

Cut notch.

Remove rootstock top.

Scion placement—The scion should fit perfectly in the stock cut, replacing the piece of bark that was removed.

Wrap the graft—Wrap from bottom to top, overlapping the tape to seal the cuts from dehydration. Tie off the wrap with a half-hitch knot or, if you use Parafilm, stretch the tape to make it stick to itself.

Aftercare—Three to four weeks later, unwrap the bud. Cut a deep notch in the rootstock stem just above the scion, to encourage the bud to grow. After several weeks, the scion will be growing out strongly. The rootstock top can now be removed completely, and the scion should be staked to avoid having it snap off due to wind or injury.

---

tissue of the plant, and looks like a small blob of white or pale-tan spongy material.) In cold weather, grafts should be left wrapped longer. Fall-grafted plants may be left wrapped until spring. Roses, apples and pears can be chip-budded in the fall; pecans are usually grafted during dormancy, in late fall or winter.

Two grafting methods

There are many methods of budding and grafting from which to choose. Two of my favorites are veneer grafting and chip budding. Veneer grafting is more likely to be successful than are most other methods, especially with difficult plant species. This is probably due to several things: the scion is relatively large, the exposed cambium area is large, and the scion is totally wrapped with tape, which conserves moisture. This method is a good one to use when learning to graft.

In veneer grafting, a thin strip of bark is removed from the side of a rootstock plant. Rootstocks can be slightly thinner than a pencil to slightly thicker than your thumb. The scion is a short (3-in.) twig. The bark is removed from the entire length of one side of the scion, and the cut side is placed against the rootstock cut, with the cambium layers, which are located just beneath the bark, aligned.

Chip budding is really just a type of veneer grafting, but uses a tiny, one-bud scion. This chip of bark replaces an identical chip removed from the rootstock stem. Once you've mastered veneer grafting, chip budding is quite easy to learn. The big advantage of budding is that you can produce two or three times as many plants from the same amount of budwood as you could by veneer grafting.

Both methods can be used at any time of year, depending on what you're grafting and assuming that the temperature remains above freezing while you're doing the work. I think the best time, however, is about a month before you want the scions to begin active growth. □

Malcolm M. Manners is assistant professor of citrus and horticulture at the Citrus Institute, Florida Southern College, Lakeland, Florida.

Training Grapes
The first four years shape a vine

by Jill Hannum

To grow into a horticulturally responsible adult, a young grapevine needs training. Its natural inclination is to sprawl all over and climb trees. You have to channel that energy, forcing the vine to take a convenient, compact form.

Training grapevines is a painstaking process, but not difficult. I learned on the job. From 1977 to 1982, in California's San Joaquin Valley, my partner and I grew 40 acres of 'Thompson Seedless' for raisins, and a small plot of European grapes, most of them delightful dessert types like 'Black Rose', 'Rish Baba' and 'Muscat of Alexandria'. I now grow many of the same varieties (but fewer vines by far) in the mountains in northern California. In my experience, the guidelines for training look complicated but become clear as soon as you take pruning shears in hand.

In the first two years of training, the goal is to encourage the growth of a strong root system and to create a trunk as fast as possible. Near the end of the second year, you start to shape the top of the plant, creating permanent arms, a process that takes two more years.

I use two training systems, which differ mainly in the location of the arms. One is head-training, with five short arms spaced evenly around the top third of the trunk. The other is cordon-training, in which the trunk forms a *T*, and the two horizontal members, called cordons, each bear five stubby arms.

There are many other training systems in use across the United States. Their merits are hard to gauge—lore and fact are scrambled together, and research keeps changing the picture. My advice is to ask your extension agent or a local grower about grape varieties suited for your area and recommended training systems. But the chances are that either head-training or cordon-training will work well for you, and in any case, the basics of training are the same for most systems.

Once a vine has been trained, you

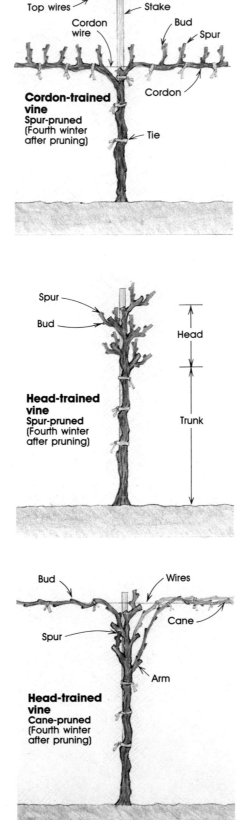

Cordon-trained vine
Spur-pruned
(Fourth winter after pruning)

Top wires — Stake
Cordon wire
Bud — Spur
Cordon
Tie

Head-trained vine
Spur-pruned
(Fourth winter after pruning)

Spur
Bud
Head
Trunk

Head-trained vine
Cane-pruned
(Fourth winter after pruning)

Bud — Wires
Spur — Cane
Arm

prune it annually to maintain its shape and control the size of its crop. There are two systems: cane-pruning, where canes are shortened to eight or more buds, and spur-pruning, where canes are shortened to stubs bearing one to three buds. Cane-pruned vines usually need more room and produce bigger crops than spur-pruned vines do. If space is tight, a head-trained, spur-pruned vine is a good choice. It takes the least room and is the only shape that requires no trellis once the vine is five or six years old.

Trellising

Grapes need support. You have to provide each vine a sturdy stake and an arbor or a trellis, which you should set when you plant so the young vine can grow undisturbed. (Some growers wait until the second year, but I think that this invites damage to the vine.) For stakes, growers here use redwood 2x2s or galvanized lightweight versions of the metal *T*-posts used for livestock fences. Almost anything will do, provided it can last five years in the ground. I bury 2 ft. of the stake, leaving 6 ft. above ground.

The trellis or arbor must bear the weight of the vine and its crop, offer the tendrils something to cling to, and let the canopy spread so the leaves get air and sunlight. If you plan to grow several vines in a row, make a commercial-style wire-strung trellis, with firmly anchored end posts, and intermediate posts spaced 10 ft. apart. Use pressure-treated wood; I recommend 4x4s for posts and 2x4s for crossarms. If your trellis is less than 30 ft. long, you can just sink the end posts deeply—3 ft. or so. Over the years, they'll lean from the weight of the vines, but not much, and you can retighten the wire periodically. For longer trellises, brace the end posts, or wire them to deadmen, which are buried anchors (they can be as simple as a length of treated wood). Space the vines 6 ft. to 10 ft. apart. A weak spur-pruned vine needs the least room; a

Hannum head-trains a third-year vine in a commercial vineyard by choosing five canes to head back and create permanent arms (facing page).

All photos: Staff; drawings: Laura B. Goodwin

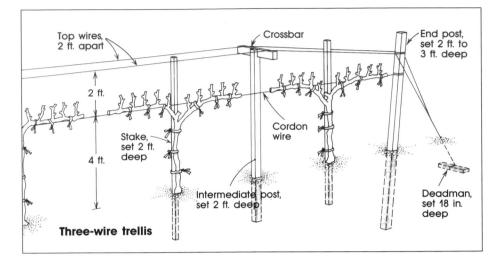

Top wires, 2 ft. apart

Crossbar

End post, set 2 ft. to 3 ft. deep

2 ft.

4 ft.

Stake, set 2 ft. deep

Cordon wire

Intermediate post, set 2 ft. deep

Deadman, set 18 in. deep

Three-wire trellis

strong cane-pruned vine, the most.

You have to match the trellis to your training system. For cordon-trained vines, I like a three-wire trellis, with a lower wire to support the cordons at a comfortable height for pruning (about 4 ft.), and the other wires 2 ft. higher and 2 ft. apart. As new growth arises from the cordon, you guide it between the top wires and then let it sprawl at will. This helps support the canes and spreads the canopy nicely. For head-trained, cane-pruned vines, dispense with the lower wire and tie the canes to the upper wires in opposing directions. A head-trained, spur-pruned vine needs no trellis, but you can use one to raise the canopy.

You can also use alternative supports, such as gates and fences. These days, I don't make my vines march in rows—I like to see them play a landscaping role. I'm training some on the side of my house, others on an arbor. I treat these vines in standard fashion, except that I train them to longer trunks.

Buying and planting

There is a great deal that can be learned about buying and planting grapevines, but this should get you started. I advise using nursery-grown vines. You can propagate your own plants easily enough, by layering or by rooting cuttings, but nursery stock will give you a year's head start. I'd try cuttings, however, if they were the only way to have a rare variety.

I've transplanted both one-year and two-year vines, with decent luck. ("Year" in this case means growing season in the nursery.) Commercial growers put out one-year vines, and many experts recommend them. You pay more for two-year vines, but where summers are arid these may transplant better than one-year vines.

I prefer to buy bare-root rather than potted plants because I can look for strong root systems. If you buy potted vines, make sure they are neither held-over culls from last year nor root-bound. If you buy mail-order, deal with a reputable nursery.

I also prefer buying unpruned vines. I

can choose plants with plump buds, not thin, scale-like buds, and with smooth, flexible canes that show no sign of shriveling or dryness. Besides, I want to do the pruning. There's something very satisfying about the two or three little snips that signal the beginning of a long relationship.

Here in northern California, I can plant anytime during the winter. If you buy vines and have to wait for spring thaw, store your plants with their roots in moist sawdust in a cool spot to keep them dormant. After you transplant the vines, be prepared to protect them from frost. New shoots are tender and easily killed. Frost rarely kills the vine, but it sets back growth.

To plant, dig a hole about 2½ ft. in diameter and 1 ft. deep, large enough to accommodate the roots without crowding or bending (but prune especially long roots rather than dig a huge hole). The heavier your soil is, the larger the hole should be. Loosening the dirt over a large area seems to be the key to success.

Set the plant at the nursery groundline, indicated by a change in color on the vine. If you buy grafted vines, as we must do in parts of California to get a rootstock resistant to phylloxera (a nasty pest also known as the grape louse), plant them with the graft union a good 2 in. above the ground. It's wise practice with any vine to avoid planting with a bud right at or just below soil level, as this is liable to produce a plague of unwanted shoots, called suckers, for years to come.

I place the vine with the main stem an inch or so from the stake at ground level and slanting slightly toward it, and backfill with the excavated dirt. I don't amend the backfill. Few soils, aside from the heaviest clays and pure sand, are too poor for grapes. My ground is wet in winter and stays that way through spring, but if you can't count on a rainstorm to settle

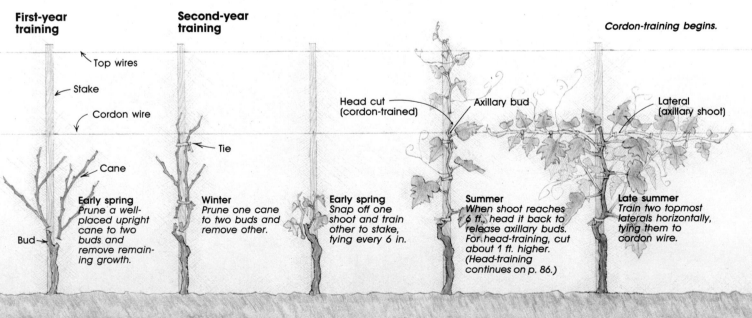

First-year training

Top wires

Stake

Cordon wire

Cane

Bud

Early spring Prune a well-placed upright cane to two buds and remove remaining growth.

Second-year training

Tie

Winter Prune one cane to two buds and remove other.

Early spring Snap off one shoot and train other to stake, tying every 6 in.

Cordon-training begins.

Head cut (cordon-trained)

Axillary bud

Lateral (axillary shoot)

Summer When shoot reaches 6 ft., head it back to release axillary buds. For head-training, cut about 1 ft. higher. (Head-training continues on p. 86.)

Late summer Train two topmost laterals horizontally, tying them to cordon wire.

the backfill soon, you should water. When the ground begins to dry out in late spring, I give each vine about 25 gal. of water every ten days, which may be too much. I plan to switch to a neighbor's schedule of 5 gal. every fourth day for new vines and double that for three-year-olds.

First-year training

Training starts right after the vine has been transplanted. The standard rule is to cut back the vine almost completely, leaving a short stem that bears just two buds. (The drawing below, which continues on p. 86, shows an overview of all the stages of training.) Leaving three or more buds tends to make a shrubby plant, and to complicate shaping a trunk. Leaving two buds lets the vine gather strength, producing stronger roots than if one bud were left. And it's less risky. If you lose one cane, the other will take over.

Choosing the two buds can be tricky, unless your plants were properly pruned at the nursery. If you have unpruned plants, they're likely to have lots of small canes. Look for a relatively strong cane with upright growth. Cut it back to two upward-facing buds. Avoid basal buds, the inconspicuous bumps found at the base of a cane. They tend to grow sideways or down at first and then turn up, making a cane with a bend, which is an unsuitable candidate for the trunk of a vine. Also try to avoid canes that grow horizontally. When you have no choice, however, choose a horizontal cane with an upward-facing bud near its base. This puts a small jog in the trunk, but doesn't weaken it much. With time, the jog will fill in and the trunk will stand straight.

Once you've selected a cane and cut it back, prune away all the remaining canes. I use bypass rather than anvil shears. They let me prune flush, which re-

This freshly transplanted vine (above left) lacks a well-placed upright cane to initiate the trunk. Hannum cuts back to a low cane with topside buds near its base (above right). She will use the shoot from one of these buds for the trunk.

moves basal buds and reduces unwanted sprouting the next season.

In the spring, if you're lucky, the vine produces two lovely green shoots. They are fast-growing, shockingly fragile and easy to injure or knock off the vine. Periodically during the spring and summer, tie the shoots to the stake to keep them off the ground and prevent wind damage. I use nursery tape for tying. It's just stretchy plastic with no adhesive, and gives as the shoots thicken, so it can't girdle them. If you tie the shoots with string or twist-ties, leave slack and make sure the shoots have room all season.

Spring can hold surprises. Sometimes one bud is dead, leaving just one shoot, which I treat very gently. Sometimes many shoots appear. I rub off all but the two I want. If I do this early, when the shoots are a few inches long, it seems to reduce the incidence of unwanted shoots sprouting from the base of the vine later.

During the growing season, I make sure the vine has enough water to pro-

mote maximum growth. With good weather, my two shoots keep growing into the fall, gradually turning woody from the base outward. At some indefinable point, perhaps when 2 ft. or 3 ft. has hardened, grape growers start calling these shoots by a new name, canes. It's a good idea to refrain from watering in the fall. If you force the canes to keep growing, they'll be tender and susceptible to cold injury. I count myself satisfied if I have two well-hardened, healthy canes halfway to the top of a 6-ft. stake by the end of the growing season. Don't be disturbed if your canes are smaller, or bigger. You're going to remove them soon anyway. Just aim for a good season's growth.

Second-year training

Since the canes of most transplanted vines fail to reach trunk height in their first season, the standard treatment is to cut them back during the following winter to force 5 ft. or more of growth the next season. I choose the healthier of the two

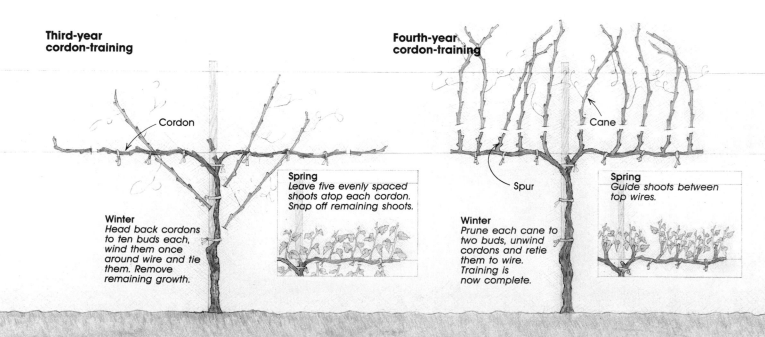

Third-year cordon-training

Cordon

Winter
Head back cordons to ten buds each, wind them once around wire and tie them. Remove remaining growth.

Spring
Leave five evenly spaced shoots atop each cordon. Snap off remaining shoots.

Fourth-year cordon-training

Cane

Spur

Winter
Prune each cane to two buds, unwind cordons and retie them to wire. Training is now complete.

Spring
Guide shoots between top wires.

canes, provided it is reasonably upright and close to the stake. I cut it back to two or three buds, and then remove the remaining cane entirely. The vine now looks very much as it did a year before, which is frustrating, but there's a crucial difference: The root system is much stronger than it was at transplanting.

When spring comes, and the new shoots have grown about 8 in. long, remove all but one. There is no need for shears; just bend the shoots away from the vine until they snap off. This makes a clean, flush break. The shoot you keep will be the trunk of the mature vine, so you want it to stay straight. As it grows, add a tie every 6 in. or so, and watch the vine diligently. With a strong root system pushing it, the shoot grows with great vigor, as much as 6 in. a week. For me, it readily grows well past the height I want in one season. If you need a longer cane than the one that forms this season, wait until winter and cut the cane at the first point where its diameter is ½ in. or more. In spring, keep the highest shoot from this cane, remove all the others, and carry on.

As the second growing season progresses, unwanted shoots may appear. Generally, they arise from buds under the bark of old wood (such shoots are called water sprouts), or from surviving basal buds. They tend to recur every year, but I find that promptly removing them reduces the problem. You may also see suckers from the rootstock or from buds just below ground level. Pull away enough soil to be able to snap them off. If allowed to develop, suckers can form hard-to-remove basal buds, which will lead to chronic suckering.

Once your chosen shoot has grown at least 1 ft. beyond the height at which you plan to shape the vine's permanent head or cordons, cut it back to that height. (That's the location of the lower wire on a

Here, Hannum is head-training a vine in its third winter. She removes all but the canes on the top third of the vine, and cuts these back to two or three buds each. This vine has made ideal growth and offers five well-spaced canes.

three-wire trellis, for a cordon-trained vine.) If they haven't yet formed, this cutting prompts new shoots, called laterals, to develop at the leaf axils of the cane. Let them develop at will, as some will contribute to the vine's mature shape. For a vine you plan to head-train, you need do no more pruning or tying this season.

If you plan to cordon-train the vine, and it is making good laterals, choose two for training. These should arise no lower than 10 in. below the wire they're to be tied to; 6 in. to 8 in. is preferable. Look for laterals that arise on opposite sides of the trunk and extend in the same plane as the trellis. If I have an otherwise good pair that is slightly out of the desired plane, I'll pull them around to the right place. To hold them horizontal, I tie the laterals very gently and loosely to the wire.

As the two laterals elongate, add ties every 12 in. or so, but leave 8 in. of the tip growing free, so it can turn upward. The books say that if the tip is tied horizontally, it will stop growing. I've never experi-

mented to see if this is true or not. Why risk it? When the laterals are at least a foot beyond the halfway point to the next vine (they may not get that far the second season), cut them back to the halfway mark. I let them grow past the intended terminus so they'll develop a healthy diameter to cut back to.

Third-year training

A cordon-trained vine starts the third season with a straight trunk topped by two horizontal canes. During the winter, cut each of these canes to ten buds or less—no longer than 3 ft. and at least ⅜ in. thick at the cut. Prune off any growth on the trunk or the canes. On a weak vine, the ⅜-in. diameter may be close to the trunk. I cut to it anyway, leaving only stubs. In this case, when spring comes, I treat the outermost shoots on each stub as I did the laterals the previous year: I tie them to the wire until they are 12 in. beyond the desired end point, then cut them back.

Once you've pruned the canes, wrap them one to one and a half times around the wire and tie them. This keeps them from flopping over when new shoots appear, which would leave the shoots pointing at the ground rather than rising and spreading as they should to get as much of the canopy in the sun as possible. It's important to remember to unwrap the canes after the growing season and retie them to the wire without any turns. Left alone, they are likely to overgrow the wire.

The aim is to establish evenly spaced shoots along each cane, which is now properly called a cordon. In spring, when the vine breaks dormancy, snap off any shoots that arise from the underside of the cordons. I keep only the shoots that arise from the top third or so of the cordons. This is largely for my convenience, but it's not necessary. In fact, the winery owners

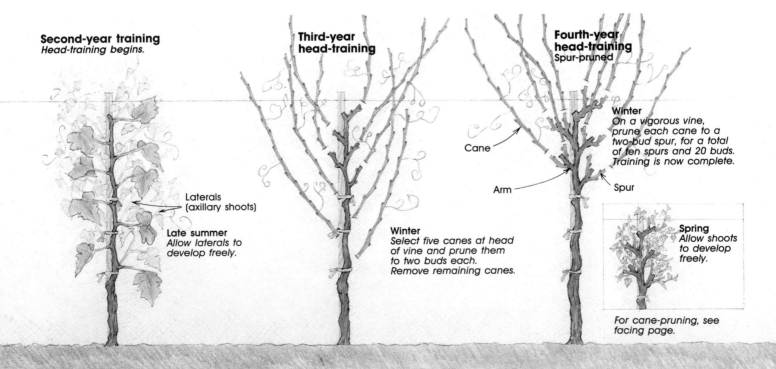

Second-year training
Head-training begins.

Laterals (axillary shoots)

Late summer
Allow laterals to develop freely.

Third-year head-training

Winter
Select five canes at head of vine and prune them to two buds each. Remove remaining canes.

Fourth-year head-training
Spur-pruned

Cane

Arm

Spur

Winter
On a vigorous vine, prune each cane to a two-bud spur, for a total of ten spurs and 20 buds. Training is now complete.

Spring
Allow shoots to develop freely.

For cane-pruning, see facing page.

for whom I sometimes prune Cabernet vines insist that I leave spurs on the bottom of the cordon. They say that these produce the biggest bunches of all.

Removing the underside shoots leaves each cordon with a topside row of five shoots spaced 6 in. to 9 in. apart. That's in theory anyway. In practice, you'll sometimes have too many top shoots, and have to break some off. On a three-wire trellis, guide the shoots, as they grow, between the top two wires. This keeps them upright and prevents their weight from twisting the cordon. In a few years, when the cordon is larger and stiffer, it will hold its own. If I see grape clusters, I remove them early to let the vine concentrate on growth.

The shoots along the cordon grow at different rates. This is usually governed by their position on the cordon—those at the base and the tip of the cordons tend to be more vigorous than those in between. It's a good idea to pinch back the most vigorous to about five leaves early in the season. This lets weaker shoots catch up.

For a head-trained vine, during the winter choose five canes spaced more or less evenly around the top third of the trunk and cut them back to two buds. These five stubs are the vine's young arms. Remove all other canes, taking care to prune flush with the trunk and destroy the basal buds.

During the next growing season, the arms produce two vigorous canes apiece, and sometimes a few grape clusters, which I remove. I also promptly remove suckers and water sprouts. Ideally, by the end of the season, I will be rewarded with ten healthy canes.

Fourth-year training

A head-trained vine is now ready to prune for production. It will get bulkier

This cordon-trained vine is in its fourth winter. Hannum is creating arms by cutting back each cane to two or three buds. Here, she removes an unwanted lateral before heading back a cane.

over the years, and bear more fruit, but its shape will not change much. You can expect something between a half-crop and a full crop the coming season.

If you're spur-pruning a vigorous vine, in the winter cut each cane back to a spur of two buds. This leaves ten spurs and 20 buds, enough for a fairly full crop. For a less vigorous vine, spur a cane on each arm to two buds and remove the remaining canes. This leaves five spurs and ten buds.

Cane-pruning is a bit more complicated. You prune the vine to a few long canes (each one bearing eight to 15 buds) and to a few spurs. The canes produce fruit this season and are removed the following winter. The spurs produce canes that will bear fruit the next year.

If I'm working with a vigorous young vine, I choose three canes evenly spaced around the top of the trunk and cut each back to about ten buds—fewer on less vigorous canes. (The following year, the vine can probably support four such

canes, and in subsequent years five, with as many as 15 buds each.) I tie these canes to the trellis wires, two in one direction, one in the other direction. It helps to wrap them one or two times around the wire before tying. If they produce a full crop, they need the support. Next I choose two or three canes for spurs and cut them to two buds each. I prune off everything except the chosen canes and spurs.

With especially weak vines, I leave only one cane, sometimes none, and cut back the best-placed canes to spurs, knowing that they will produce good canes the following year.

Since cordon-trained vines are generally spur-pruned, they are relatively easy to manage from the fourth year on. In the winter, take off any canes that escaped your notice and grew on the underside of the cordon. Then cut the canes on the topside to spurs. The next year, these spurs become the cordon's arms, and a vigorous vine can support two spurs at each arm—but then you're pruning, not training.

A last word

There is no denying that grapes take labor. You can't just plant them and come back for the harvest. But I enjoy the effort more than almost any other garden chore. Perhaps that's only because I no longer need to deal with 40 acres of them, but I don't think so. It's satisfying to train and prune grapes. You have a productive vine in three to four years, and it can be a flight of your own fancy or a match for commercial vines. You'll also have more grapes than you ever thought you wanted, only to discover that it's not quite enough. Which is a great excuse to plant more grapes. ☐

Jill Hannum lives in Yorkville, California.

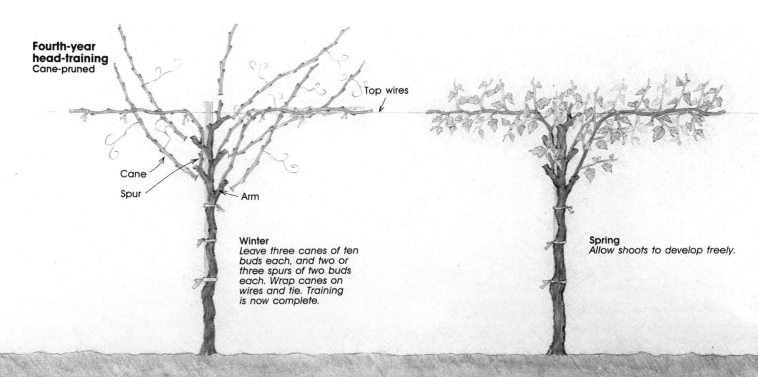

Fourth-year head-training
Cane-pruned

Top wires

Cane

Spur

Arm

Winter
Leave three canes of ten buds each, and two or three spurs of two buds each. Wrap canes on wires and tie. Training is now complete.

Spring
Allow shoots to develop freely.

Pruning Grapevines
The goals are convenience and consistent crops

Author Greensfelder cane-prunes a five-year-old grapevine in a commercial vineyard. She'll leave four shortened canes, each bearing eight to 14 buds, and five much shorter remnants bearing two buds each.

by Liese Greensfelder

had countless calls from gardeners for help pruning grapevines and saw a lot of shapeless, unproductive plants during my four years as an extension agent. The gardener either had inherited a neglected vine and couldn't make sense of the mess, or had misconceptions about pruning (the most common being that grapevines are like hedges and pruning is like shearing), or had no idea how to prune grapevines. Though I generally could fix the vine and explain grape pruning in 20 minutes, it still seemed like magic to some gardeners.

In practice, grape pruning is simple. In the winter, you remove much of the previous season's growth and some older wood, aiming to leave the vine with a desirable shape and enough buds to produce good growth and grapes the next season. In the field, an experienced pruner can teach you just about everything you need to know in less than half an hour. After a dozen vines, you'll have seen most of the choices you'll ever face and learned the basic principles. The next best source of information is *General Viticulture* (A.J. Winkler et al.; University of California Press, 1095 Essex St., Richmond, CA 94801; 1974; $30), the grape grower's bible, which devotes a 50-page chapter to grape pruning. I can't take you into the field, and I don't have 50 pages, so first I'm going to talk about the basics—how grapevines grow and fruit, why we prune them, how to look ahead a year while you prune—and then I'm going to prune a few paper vines. That's enough to get you started, whether your vines are well trained or as undisciplined as the Katzenjammer kids.

Basics

We prune grapevines for convenience—to keep the vines a manageable size. Left unpruned, grapevines run rampant. The reason lies in the way they grow (see drawing at right). Grapevines bear their leaves and fruit on slender woody canes that reach their full length in one growing season. At the base of each leaf is a fuzzy prominent bud, which gives rise the next year to a new cane. The parts of a grapevine that are more than a year old have dormant buds hidden under the bark, but in any season only a few of these produce canes. So an unpruned vine extends farther from the trunk each year, with a core of old nonproductive wood and a fringe of fruit-bearing canes. In a few years, a vigorous vine can extend 40 ft. It's little wonder I get so many calls for help.

Pruning aims to forcibly restrain the grapevine. It confines the old wood to

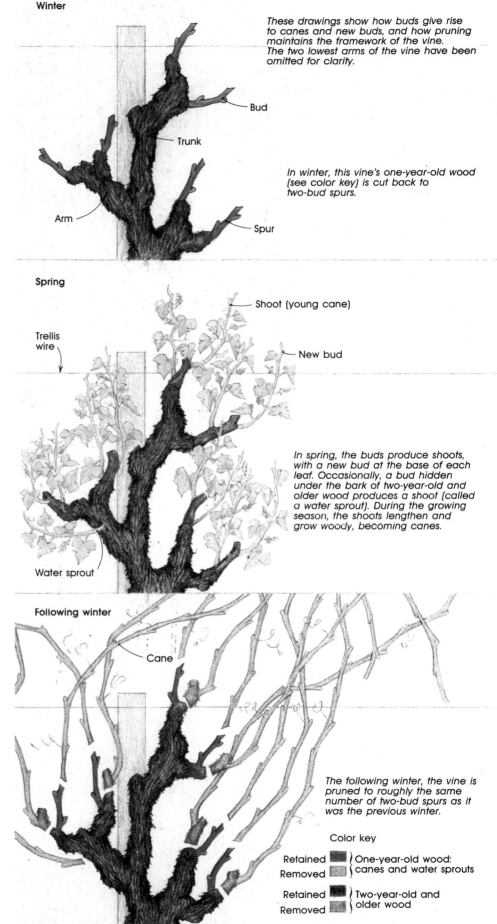

An overview of one season's growth and pruning
Winter

These drawings show how buds give rise to canes and new buds, and how pruning maintains the framework of the vine. The two lowest arms of the vine have been omitted for clarity.

Bud

Trunk

In winter, this vine's one-year-old wood (see color key) is cut back to two-bud spurs.

Arm

Spur

Spring

Shoot (young cane)

Trellis wire

New bud

In spring, the buds produce shoots, with a new bud at the base of each leaf. Occasionally, a bud hidden under the bark of two-year-old and older wood produces a shoot (called a water sprout). During the growing season, the shoots lengthen and grow woody, becoming canes.

Water sprout

Following winter

Cane

The following winter, the vine is pruned to roughly the same number of two-bud spurs as it was the previous winter.

Color key

Retained — One-year-old wood:
Removed — canes and water sprouts

Retained — Two-year-old and
Removed — older wood

All illustrations: Laura B. Goodwin

playing the role of a framework, generally in the shape of a straight trunk with two to five arms, or a trunk that bends and runs horizontally, with the horizontal portion, called a cordon, topped by short arms at regular intervals. The framework has several purposes: to hold the new growth high, so the canes can form a generous canopy without trailing on the ground; to see that the new growth arises on one level, so the canes are equal in strength; and to space the new growth, so each cane has a place in the canopy. New vines need to undergo four years of training to put the framework in place (see "Training Grapes" on pp. 82-87). Pruning then maintains the shape, shortening the one-year-old wood to minimize the inevitable extension of the vine, and correcting overextension by shortening or cutting away arms and replacing them with the canes (called water sprouts) that arise from old wood (photos at right). With good pruning, a vine can hold much the same shape for 40 years. Only the proportions change, as the trunk and arms grow thicker (and more picturesque).

Besides maintaining the grapevine in a manageable and useful shape, pruning has the equally important aim of ensuring that the vine produces consistent crops of good-size berries year after year. Grape canes bear leaves and fruit in a characteristic way. The leaves are alternate, originating from nodes spaced at roughly equal intervals. Grape clusters grow opposite some leaves. How many clusters a cane produces is largely a matter of the grape variety. Generally, the range is two to five clusters—some varieties bear two, some five. An unpruned vine, which may have 150 buds, can bear 300 or more clusters, too many for a high-quality crop. Pruning drastically reduces a vine's bud total, to as few as 14 and as many as 60, depending on the variety and the training system. This means that the energy stored in the roots and old wood of the vine fuels fewer buds than usual. The result is more and bigger leaves, which in turn means more photosynthesis and more energy for the grape clusters. Many gardeners think grapevines are lazy and need the shock of pruning to fruit well. In fact, the opposite is true. The grapevine is eager to make grapes, and pruning saves it from bearing too many.

For a vine to produce consistent crops, pruning has to respect its capacity—the number of clusters the vine can mature properly. If a vine has a capacity of 28 clusters but is allowed to bear 40, the crop is likely to be low-quality, and the canes and leaves will be smaller than usual. Many canes will not mature, and their tips may shrivel and die back. Since the vine expends too much energy on making grapes, it cannot store enough for good future production. The following year,

Greensfelder removes an overextended arm (top) and replaces it with a water sprout, pruned to two buds (one is hidden in the view above).

its capacity will be considerably lower. A different problem arises when a vine is pruned severely. If its capacity is 28 clusters and it carries only ten, the vine will concentrate on regaining its former size. It will make rampant growth but neglect to make fruitful buds. The next season, many canes will be barren or carry fewer, smaller clusters than usual. (Overwatering and overfertilizing can also provoke vigorous cane growth and unfruitful buds.)

While pruning is the most widely practiced method of influencing the number of clusters a vine bears, mainly because it's convenient, thinning the crop by removing clusters has the same desirable effects on berry size and quality. It's possible to combine the advantages of both practices by leaving more buds on the vine than usual and thinning early in the season to get the right number of clusters. The result will be bigger, sweeter grapes, without any loss of capacity the next season. In this article, I'll focus on pruning, but you might consider experimenting with thinning once you have some confidence in the way you're pruning your vines.

Pruning

Grapevines are pruned during the dormant season, anytime from leaf fall until the buds begin to open in the spring. If you live where spring frosts sometimes damage fruit crops, it's a good idea to wait and prune grapevines late in the winter, which will delay budbreak a few days to a week.

There are two pruning styles: spur-pruning and cane-pruning. The difference lies mainly in how you cut chosen canes. In spur-pruning, you cut them back to two or three buds, leaving 3-in. to 6-in. remnants called spurs, and remove all other canes. To be a candidate for spur-pruning, a grape variety must have fruitful buds near the base of its canes. This excludes some varieties, notably 'Thompson Seedless', the predominant supermarket grape in the United States, as well as 'Concord' and 'Concord'-type varieties. In cane-pruning, you cut canes back to eight to 14 buds, which leaves 2-ft. to 4-ft. remnants. If you're not sure about a variety, you can cane-prune most of it and spur-prune one or two arms as an experiment.

Before I prune, I look the vine over to identify the canes and water sprouts, and to check their location and health. I make sense of the usual tangle by looking first at the oldest portions, the trunk and the arms, because they're easy to distinguish, then I move outward to the newest portions, the canes. You can tell the parts by some simple features. Wood three years old and older has shaggy, thick bark and no visible buds. Two-year-old wood is usually just starting to get shaggy, lacks visible buds and gives rise to canes. One-year-old wood (canes and water sprouts) has a smooth, reddish-brown surface and prominent buds at the nodes. I note water sprouts carefully, as they may prove handy to replace a weak or overextended arm. I also note suspect canes. For example, overlong canes with widely spaced buds and short canes with closely spaced buds are liable to produce weak or unfruitful canes the next season. I also avoid canes that have not matured to the tip, or have died back. When in doubt, I lop off a bit of the tip and look at the cut. If I see green, I know the cane is healthy. Occasionally I see canes that are more oval than round in cross section. Since these bear weak buds, I avoid them, too.

I also try to match the number of buds I leave with the vine's capacity. Here experience helps, but I can give you a few tips. First, see how the last pruning affected the vine. If an otherwise healthy, well-fed and watered vine makes short canes, chances are you overestimated its capacity and left too many buds. (If the grapes were small, that's another indication.) If you left too few buds, you're likely to see long, thick canes, and oversized leaves. Here's a very rough rule of thumb: Leave between 12 and 24 buds on spur-pruned vines, and between 40 and 60 buds on cane-pruned vines. That will get you started, and in a year or two you'll have enough experience to adjust the bud total.

I find small loppers the most convenient pruning tool. With 18-in. handles and short blades, my pair is easy to move around and through the vines, and I can cut

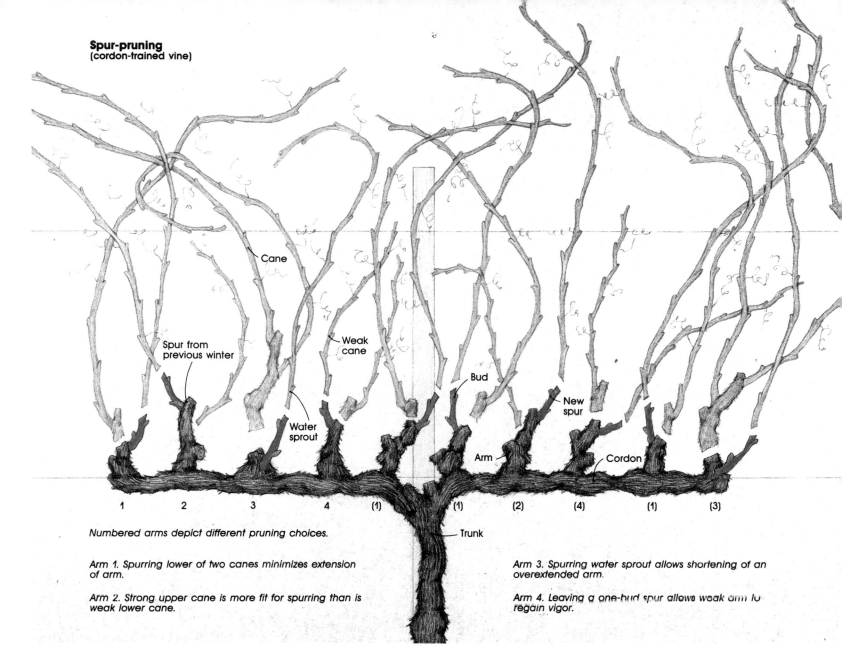

Spur-pruning
(cordon-trained vine)

Cane

Spur from
previous winter

Weak
cane

Water
sprout

Bud

New
spur

Arm

Cordon

1   2   3   4   (1)   (1)   (2)   (4)   (1)   (3)

Numbered arms depict different pruning choices.

Trunk

Arm 1. Spurring lower of two canes minimizes extension of arm.

Arm 2. Strong upper cane is more fit for spurring than is weak lower cane.

Arm 3. Spurring water sprout allows shortening of an overextended arm.

Arm 4. Leaving a one-bud spur allows weak arm to regain vigor.

wood an inch or so in diameter. I've used long-handled loppers, but they're more awkward in a tangle of canes, and it's not as easy to make precision cuts with them. If you don't have long- or short-handled loppers, you can get by with a pair of hand shears for most of the cuts and a small pruning saw for the larger cuts.

Spur-pruning

I'll start by spur-pruning the cordon-trained vine in the drawing above. This is a well-trained, five-year-old vine, with the cordons level on the wire. The arms arise every 8 in. to 12 in. along the cordons. The vine is not a vigorous cultivar, with canes only 2 ft. to 3 ft. long. Another cultivar, for example 'Concord' or 'French Colombard', might have canes 10 ft. or even 15 ft. long.

On an arm with two canes, such as arm 1, you have two pruning choices. You can cut back the higher cane to two

buds and remove the other, leaving the arm a good 8 in. longer. You want, however, to hold the vine to approximately the same size year after year, so the logical choice is to cut back the lower cane to two buds, remove everything above it and leave the arm only 4 in. longer.

There is one case where I pay no attention to minimizing the growth of the arms. I frequently see canes of different vigor on the same arm. I choose the stronger cane to spur, regardless of its position. Arm 2 is an example. In this case, I used the upper cane. I avoided the weak one because its buds will grow poorly the next season. If you use the weak cane to make a spur, you weaken the arm.

Arm 3 is overextended. To shorten it, I took advantage of the water sprout at its base. I spurred the water sprout and removed the arm.

Since this vine is not a vigorous variety, I cut back to spurs of only one or two

buds. I try to match the number of buds to the strength of the arm. On vigorous arms, such as 1, 2 and 3, I left two-bud spurs. On arm 4, which has short, weak canes, I left a one-bud spur. This gives the weak arm a chance to gain ground on its neighbors. If the vine were stronger, I would have left two or three buds on each spur, in effect increasing the crop by one-third.

I judge the vigor of each arm by noting the thickness and length of its canes. Often there are pronounced differences. Vigor declines with poor health and overcropping, but also with position. Buds on the highest parts of the vine usually are the first to start growth in the spring. The early jump produces shoots that overtop those that start later. Since canes that are exposed to plenty of sunlight are more vigorous (and fruitful) than canes that get less, eventually the lower portions of the vine weaken and stop producing buds. To avoid this, it's critical to train and

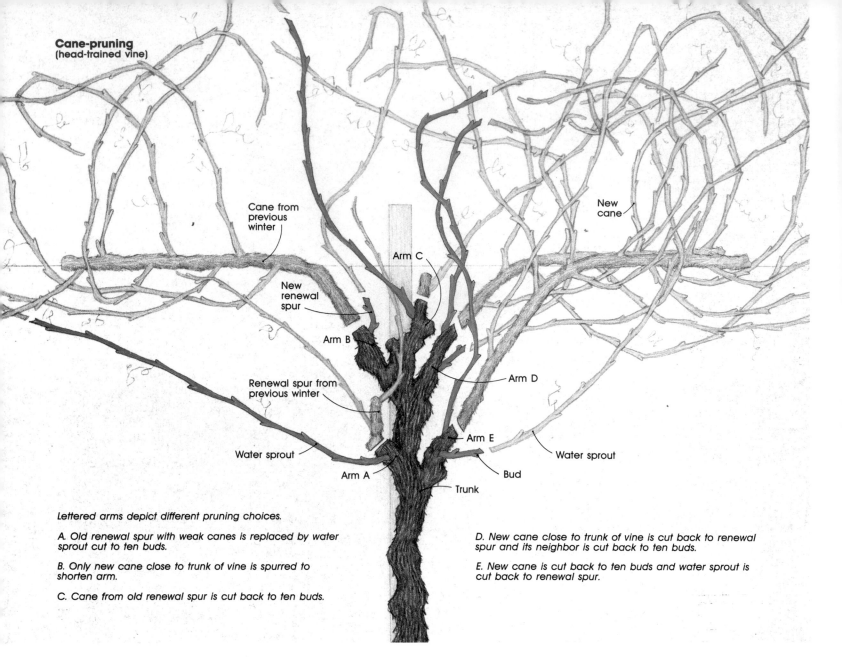

Cane-pruning
(head-trained vine)

Cane from previous winter

New renewal spur

Arm C

Arm B

Renewal spur from previous winter

Arm D

New cane

Arm E

Water sprout

Water sprout

Arm A

Bud

Trunk

Lettered arms depict different pruning choices.

A. Old renewal spur with weak canes is replaced by water sprout cut to ten buds.

B. Only new cane close to trunk of vine is spurred to shorten arm.

C. Cane from old renewal spur is cut back to ten buds.

D. New cane close to trunk of vine is cut back to renewal spur and its neighbor is cut back to ten buds.

E. New cane is cut back to ten buds and water sprout is cut back to renewal spur.

prune a vine so that the new growth is close to the same level. A common mistake is training the cordon in a bow shape, with a sagging middle and high points at either end.

When cutting back a cane, I make a slanting cut ¼ in. above a bud. Any closer than this and the bud may dry out. The slant should angle away from the bud so that dew and rain will not run down the spur into the bud. When grapevines are pruned in the month or so before they leaf out, they often bleed, that is, they ooze a clear fluid from the pruning wounds. Although no one has ever shown that heavy bleeding is harmful to vine growth or crop production, I try to prune weak vines before there's a chance of bleeding. I don't worry about bleeding in normal, vigorous vines, but I'm careful to slant the cuts on the spurs properly. A bud that's continually wet with this fluid may start to decay if the weather turns warm.

At the base of water sprouts and canes is a ring of buds that generally are small and unfruitful, and remain dormant unless the buds above them are injured or fail to grow. I don't count them in the bud total, and when I remove a water sprout or a cane entirely, I make sure I destroy them. I hold the cutting blade of the loppers against the old wood, as far down the cane as possible, and try to take all the basal buds.

Cane-pruning

In cane-pruning, you leave the vine with roughly 40 to 60 buds, most of them on a few canes, and the rest on two-bud spurs called renewal spurs. With canes that bear eight to 14 buds each, tied in both directions on a trellis, a cane-pruned vine takes more room and yields bigger crops than does a spur-pruned vine. It also produces a thicket of canes that looks daunting to a new pruner. The five-year-old

head-trained vine in the drawing above looks like a jungle, but don't be intimidated—you can sort out what's what.

Last winter's pruning left three 10-bud canes, and during the past growing season canes arose from many but not all of their buds. I also left renewal spurs close to the trunk of the vine on arm A and arm C, with the aim of producing canes that I can use now to avoid overextending the framework of the vine.

My goal this winter was to leave well-placed renewal spurs and four canes, one more than last year (last season the vine was too young to carry a full crop). I found strong canes on each arm, with the exception of arm A. There, the renewal spur left last year produced two weak canes and a strong water sprout. I cut the water sprout to ten buds and removed the growth above it. I wanted two canes on each side of the vine, so I needed one more on the left. At arm B, the cane left last winter produced a new cane from its first bud, but no new canes from the next few buds. I chose to make a renewal spur here and look elsewhere for a second cane. At arm C, the renewal spur left last year produced two good canes. I cut one back to ten buds and removed the growth above it. This finished the left side of the vine.

On the right side, I left two canes and two renewal spurs. At arm D, the cane left last year produced good new canes from its first two buds. I made a renewal spur from the new cane closest to the trunk, and cut the other new cane to ten buds. At arm E, the cane left last year produced only one new cane near its base. I cut the new cane back to ten buds and made a renewal spur from the water sprout below it. This finished the right side of the vine.

In all, I left four canes and three well-placed renewal spurs. I would have preferred to have left two more renewal spurs for insurance. You can't count on every bud to produce good canes. But, with luck, next winter I can add more renewal spurs. For example, next season the ten-bud canes I left at arms A and C could produce new canes from their first few buds, and next winter I'd be able to leave a renewal spur and a ten-bud cane on each. If the vine shows enough vigor, I could also add a fifth cane by treating the ten-bud cane on arm C in the same fashion.

Here's a good trick for vines like this one, where you have to bend a cane into place to tie it to a trellis: Hold the cane with your hands over adjacent buds. Push on the length of cane between the buds with your thumbs until you hear slight cracking noises. This makes a permanent curve. By cracking the cane for as many lengths as necessary, you can bend it in any direction. Practice this technique on pruned-off canes before trying it on the vine—and use restraint. If you push too hard, the cane will break. Furthermore, don't try this when the temperature is below freezing. The canes will be too brittle.

Replacement

The arms of your vines eventually will need shortening or replacement. Some will grow longer every year, some will weaken and stop producing canes. For cordon-trained vines, I try to replace arms when they exceed 10 in. in length. For vines trained to other systems, I try to replace arms before their diameter is much larger than an inch or two. This not only keeps the vine growing from vigorous new wood, it also helps keep pruning wounds small. If you let an arm grow larger before removing it, the wound provides a good entryway into the vine for wood-rotting fungi and bacteria.

When an arm needs replacing or shortening, I look for a nearby water sprout. Sometimes I cut it back to a one-bud spur and prune the arm normally.

Last year's pruning left a spur and a cane on the bottom arm to the right of the post (top). The first five buds of the cane produced little useful growth, while the spur produced three good canes. Greensfelder cuts one back to ten buds, another to two buds, removes the third, and cuts off last year's cane, shortening the arm (above).

The next winter, I check the spur. If it has produced a sturdy cane, I use the cane to replace the arm. If I can't find a well-placed water sprout, I sometimes try to provoke the vine into making one by leaving fewer buds on an arm than I normally would. Often this trick revives dormant buds on old wood.

I don't use wound dressing when I remove arms or make other large cuts. Dressings invariably crack, allowing moisture to seep under them and accumulate. Rather than protect the wound, a dressing may create an ideal environment for wood-rotting organisms. Let the vine heal itself. It will rapidly plug small wounds with its own gummy wound dressing.

In states with Eutypa, the fungus that causes "dead arm," large pruning wounds should immediately be painted with a solution of benomyl. (Eutypa has been reported in California, New York, Michigan, and several other states and countries.) Benomyl is registered for this use in California, but you'll need to check your own state's regulations before using it.

A last word

If a vine has been properly trained and pruned, it reads like a map. Once you learn to interpret it, you know what to do. A neglected, overgrown vine is harder to read, but the basics of pruning still apply, and you usually can restore it to a manageable, productive shape. □

Liese Greensfelder was a farm advisor with the University of California Extension Service. She now lives near Nevada City, California.

Index

A

Abeliophyllum distichum, propagating, 72-74
Alyssum *(Lobularia maritima),* seed treatment for, 18
Annuals:
    deadheading, cutting back explained, 64-67
    pruning timetable, 66-67
Auxin, defined, 28
Azaleas *(Rhododendron* spp.), propagating, 73

B

Banded cuttings, propagation by, 26-28
Bassuk, Nina, and Brian Maynard, on banded cuttings, 26-28
Begonias, seeding, 8, 10
Birch, paper *(Betula papyrifera),* banded cuttings from, 27
Blanching, described, 27
Buchanan, Rita, on starting seeds, 8-13
Bugbee, Bruce, on storing seeds, 19-21

C

Calendulas, seeding, 8
California poppies *(Eschscholzia californica),* seed treatment for, 18
Carney, Nancy:
    on dividing perennials, 68-71
    on dividing suckering shrubs, 72-75
    on selecting shrubs and trees, 33-35
Chip budding. *See* Grafting.
Cleome, seed treatment for, 18
Clethra *(Clethra alnifolia),* propagating, 72-74
Coleus:
    seeding, 9
    standardizing, 47
Container gardening, with standards, 48
Containers:
    growing trees in, 40-42
    for seed storage, 20-21
    for seeded pots, 9
Cook, Alan D., on pruning shrubs, 50-53
Copper, as root inhibitor, 40-42
Cosmos, seed treatment for, 18
Cucumbers, seeding, 8
Cutting back, discussed, 65-67

D

Deadheading, discussed, 65-67
Delphinium *(Delphinium* spp.), seeding, 9
Desiccants, for seed storage, 20
Deutzia *(Deutzia gracilis),* propagating, 74
DiSabato-Aust, Tracy, on deadheading and summer pruning, 64-67
Disbudding, discussed, 65-67

E

Eddison, Sydney, on moving shrubs, 76-77
Etiolation, described, 26-28

F

Fertilizers, for seedlings, 10
Flowers, deadheading, disbudding explained, 64-67
Forsythia *(Forsythia* spp.), x *intermedia,* propagating, 73, 74

G

General Viticulture (Winkler), source for, 89
Geraniums *(Pelargonium* spp.), standardizing, 47
Gibberellic acid:
    source for, 18
    using, 18
Grafting:
    care of dormant-grafted trees, 79
    chip budding, 80-81
    resources for supplies, 79
    tips for, 79-81
    veneer grafting, 80-81
Grapes:
    books on, 89
    growing, 82-87, 88-93
Grapevines, pruning, 88-93
Greensfelder, Liese, on pruning grapevines, 88-93

H

Hannum, Jill, on training grapes, 82-87
Hibiscus *(Hibiscus* spp.), standardizing, 47
Home Orchard Society, address of, 79
Hornbeam, European *(Carpinus betulus),* banded cuttings from, 27-28
Hydrangea, oakleaf *(Hydrangea quercifolia):*
    growing, 77
    moving, 76-77

K

Kerria *(Kerria japonica),* propagating, 72, 73, 74-75

L

Legumes, seed-storage cautions for, 21

M

Manners, Malcolm M., on grafting, 78-81
Maple, sugar *(Acer saccharum),* banded cuttings from, 27
Martin, Tovah, on standardizing, 47-49
Maynard, Brian. *See* Bassuk, Nina.
Moisture, and seed viability, 19-20
Morris, B.J., on propagating perennials from cuttings, 22-25
Myrtle *(Myrtus communis):*
    sources for, 49
    standardizing, 47-49

N

North American Fruit Explorers, address of, 79
Nursery stock, selecting healthy plants, 32-35

O

Oak, red *(Quercus rubra),* banded cuttings from, 27

The 21 articles in this book originally appeared in *Fine Gardening* magazine.
The date of first publication, issue number and page numbers for each article are given below.

If you enjoyed this book, you're going to love our magazine.

A year's subscription to *Fine Gardening* brings you the kind of hands-on information you found in this book, and much more. In issue after issue—six times a year—you'll find articles on nurturing specific plants, landscape design, fundamentals and building structures. Expert gardeners will share their knowledge and techniques with you. They will show you how to apply their knowledge in your own backyard. Filled with detailed illustrations and full-color photographs, *Fine Gardening* will inspire you to create and realize your dream garden!

To subscribe, just fill out one of the attached subscription cards or call us at 1-203-426-8171. And as always, your satisfaction is guaranteed, or we'll give you your money back.

Taunton
BOOKS & VIDEOS
for fellow enthusiasts

The Taunton Press 63 S. Main Street, P.O. Box 5506, Newtown, CT 06470-5506